OVERCOME
YOUR
VILLAINS

HEATHER MONAHAN

OVERCOME YOUR VILLAINS

Mastering Your Beliefs,
Actions, and Knowledge to
Conquer Any Adversity

HarperCollins
Leadership

AN IMPRINT OF HARPERCOLLINS

Published by HarperCollins Leadership, an imprint of HarperCollins Focus LLC.

Any internet addresses, phone numbers, or company or product information printed
in this book are offered as a resource and are not intended in any way to be or to imply
an endorsement by HarperCollins Leadership, nor does HarperCollins Leadership
vouch for the existence, content, or services of these sites, phone numbers,
companies, or products beyond the life of this book.

ISBN 978-1-4002-2558-3 (eBook)
ISBN 978-1-4002-2557-6 (HC)
ISBN 978-1-4002-2560-6 (TP)

Library of Congress Control Number: 2021942686

Printed in the United States of America
22 23 24 25 LSC 10 9 8 7 6 5 4 3 2 1

To my son, Dylan, who is my biggest champion,
cheerleader, and example.
Every time I doubted myself,
I only had to look to you.
I am eternally grateful for your support
and belief in me.

Contents

OVERCOME
YOUR
VILLAINS

Note to the Reader

Thank you for taking the time to read this book. I hope it helps you in some way. If there is any chance you can share it with someone who can benefit from it and leave a review, it would mean the world to me! No one succeeds alone, and that includes me. I am grateful for your help!

—Heather Monahan

CHAPTER 1

A New Me

"I got fired."

Three words I never imagined I would say.

Three words I was too embarrassed to say to my family and friends.

Three words that changed my life—forever—in ways I had no way of predicting.

Some people describe being fired as a "humbling experience." That's not how I would describe it. *Maddening, shocking, psychotic* are all words that instantly come to mind when I look back on that terrible moment.

And what made it all that and more was how it all went down.

It might be a little easier to understand if I give you some backstory first. I grew up poor. My childhood was not one I like to sit around and reminisce about. In some ways this has been a blessing, because I learned to be driven like no other. But in other ways, this has been a holdback. For much of my life, I was driven to chase a paycheck more than anything. All I knew was I didn't want to be poor—I didn't want to struggle. I didn't want the kids I dreamed I would have someday to grow up in a trailer, as I did.

That feeling of standing in the grocery checkout line and realizing you would have to put back half of the items on the belt because you didn't have enough money pained me. Oddly, some people would have no problem with that. For some reason, however, when it happened to me, it ripped my heart out. The shame I felt thinking others were looking down on me, realizing I couldn't buy what I wanted and had to operate differently, was long-lasting.

Once you feel like that, there's a really good chance you will do anything in your power to never feel that way again. And that's exactly how I responded.

WORKING MY WAY UP

I started delivering newspapers at ten years old, then busing tables at a diner, then working the front counter and drive-thru windows at fast-food restaurants, then waiting tables and eventually bartending my way through college. My dream was to graduate and join a sales team. To be completely honest, I didn't just dream of joining a sales team—I desperately wanted to join a sales team. Not because I felt a passion or excitement to work for a business, but because I quickly learned that the owners of the nicest cars in the parking lot where I slung drinks were always *salespeople*.

They were the ones who left the biggest tips. *They* were the ones who had the nicest houses. *They* were the ones who had enough money to buy the most expensive suits, dresses, and shoes.

And they *never* had to put their groceries back.

I joined a top winery's sales team as soon as I graduated, and I flat outworked everyone else—even the old-timers. It didn't take long before I became the top salesperson and was promoted to brand manager.

It also didn't take long after getting promoted that my new boss started sexually harassing me. I was too afraid to take on the company, too afraid to fight for what I knew was right, so I quit. I aggressively put myself out there looking for another sales job while bartending on the side.

At a networking event a couple of weeks later, I met a man who stood out from the rest of the crowd, and I decided to chat him up. He told me I should go to work for him, and I told him he wouldn't be able to afford me. When he asked me how much I expected to be paid, I told him $75,000—never imagining he would pay anyone he just met at a networking event that kind of salary.

"You start in the morning," he told me.

I was of course excited by this stroke of good fortune—I walked into the event a part-time bartender and walked out newly employed with a $75,000 salary. What I didn't realize at the time was that I had left a lot of money on the table. I had undersold myself. This was something I would do again many times in my career.

When you don't see your own
worth, others won't see it either.
People pay you what *you*
believe you are worth.

I later learned that this man was worth many millions of dollars, and he saw potential in me. I quickly became his top seller, and he groomed me to become his partner. In my early twenties, I moved by myself across the country to take his $25 million property and turn it into a $55 million property in just under three years. I finally had some money. I had established a reputation for generating revenue like few others in the industry.

Still, I wasn't satisfied. Growing up poor had lit a fire in me that grew and grew until it consumed me. I needed more revenues, more room for growth, a higher ladder to climb, a bigger salary, more commissions.

I took my cash and my reputation and moved to Florida to go to work for a publicly traded radio company. It was a bigger company than the one I had been working for, with more revenues and far more upside potential. I pitched myself for a job that didn't exist and was awarded VP of Sales. Based on my performance, I was quickly promoted two more times and ultimately named chief revenue officer.

I was one of only two women on the executive team, and I was as proud as I could be. I had finally arrived. There was just one problem: the other woman on the executive team seemed to despise me—and she was the CEO's daughter.

Instead of engaging this woman in battle, I decided to ignore the office politics and focus on growing revenues, which I did by leaps and bounds. When I started at the company, we were billing $100 million annually. Two and a half years after I was named chief revenue officer, that number had doubled to more than $200 million annually. Much of this increase was the direct result of my own efforts.

I had the house, the car, the nice clothes, the fat cushion of cash in my bank account. I had made my dream come true. I had it all.

And then I was fired.

In an instant, I went from being the hero who had more than doubled the company's revenue, had won countless awards, had been promoted three times, and had been named one of the most influential women in radio just weeks earlier.

This was not a "humbling experience."

This was a horrific moment that left me under a weighted blanket with a bottle of chardonnay attached to my wrist. This was the lowest of the lows of my life, a grown-up version of getting your heart broken in high school. You thought you had it all figured out, you were so happy—on top of the world—only to find out you were fooling yourself all along.

That was exactly it: I had been fooling myself.

All the while that woman was hating me and nursing her apparent desire to eradicate me from the company. You see, when her father became ill and needed to step down as CEO, he elevated his only daughter to the position of interim CEO. And she tortured me. I can't lie—the way this villain treated me made me feel miserable. But I refused to buckle—I wouldn't let her get the best of me. I refused to show any weakness.

Here's just one example. I would be sitting in the conference room—usually the only other woman in the room, surrounded by male colleagues—as the villain would walk in. She would go up to each person at the table, one by one, saying hello and even hugging some. Then she would walk right by me as if I didn't exist.

Those days were tough. They were tough because by ignoring me, she was signaling to everyone else that I didn't matter. I was invisible. This feeling of being ignored really got to me, and it became worse over time. And every time I allowed this to occur, I could feel her getting stronger as I got weaker. I was like Alice in Wonderland, shrinking away to nothing after taking a swig from a bottle labeled "Drink Me."

I hated that feeling that I didn't exist.

Things had gotten so bad that, the night before I knew she would be in a meeting with me, I would start to panic. What would I do when she would inevitably ignore me again? I desperately needed my paycheck, so I couldn't do what I most wanted to do: tell her off.

What could I do?

What I hadn't realized was that allowing her to continue to ignore me was not only chipping away at my self-confidence, it was building hers. And all other executives and managers could see it. The rest of the team looked at me differently. Everyone had always seen me as a tremendously confident high-performer—but I was starting to shrink in front of their very eyes.

I was becoming nothing.

I finally had enough of this game. I decided that while I couldn't tell her off, I could make sure she and everyone else in the meeting knew I was there. To get ready for this moment, I practiced exactly what I was going to say in my mirror at home. The morning of the meeting, I picked a red outfit, a power color that allows me to feel my best, and I did my hair and took some extra time to look good because I knew it would turn my self-confidence up a notch.

I wanted to stand tall and exude confidence, and with all my preparations completed, I knew I would.

I had reached a point where nothing was worth allowing me to feel like a B-rated version of myself. I *wasn't* nothing. I had delivered millions of dollars' worth of business to the company for years. I deserved to be seen and heard. To put the icing on my confidence cake, I played my "Fire Me Up!" playlist as I drove to the office.

I showed up to the meeting and chatted everyone up. Many people complimented me on my red dress—I smiled and thanked them. It was game on.

Then, in came the interim CEO, my new boss—the villain. She walked from person to person as she always did, and passed by me as she always did. She sat at the head of the table where she always sat. That's when I made my move.

I raised my hand and said, "Good morning! You must have missed me! I'm down here and excited to be here!" I gave her a big smile and a wave.

I wasn't being mean or disrespectful, but in that moment, I was building my confidence. And I could see that hers was being chipped away.

The reality is that, in any moment,
you are either building your
confidence or chipping away at it by
the actions you take or don't take.

If my new boss had wanted to build her confidence back up, she could have simply said, "Good morning, Heather, thank you for understanding that it wasn't intentional. Glad you are here. Now, let's begin our meeting."

She didn't say anything though. She hadn't seen that one coming. I saw a few of the men at the table shoot glances to one another and even saw one of them try to hold back a laugh. *I had let it be known, loud and clear, I would no longer be ignored.*

That was it. The game ended right then and there, or so I thought.

Looking back, I believe this was the moment when the villain decided to get rid of me for good. Within a few months, I was gone.

I'm sure you know the saying "When one door closes, another door opens." That's not how I saw it—I was in a total panic. My source of income had been suddenly and irrevocably cut off. Not only that, I had signed a noncompete agreement when I became chief revenue officer, which prohibited me from taking a position with a competitor for one year after I left the company. This meant that I couldn't leverage my vast network of connections in the industry—for the next year, I would have to find some other way to generate income.

And I needed income. There's another part of the story I neglected to tell you. When I was fired, I was a single mom with a ten-year-old son, Dylan.

*While you may be expendable,
you are never replaceable.*

There's no one else in the universe like you. I didn't realize this at the time, but today—as I write these words—it is crystal clear. You have the ability and opportunity to take your unique skills and attributes anywhere you want. Just because you have been successful in one lane doesn't mean that you can't succeed in another.

Getting fired was painful and heartbreaking. That day I truly felt I had lost everything. What I didn't realize was that while they could take away my paycheck, everything else stayed with me. No one can ever take away your reputation, your experiences, your network, and your talents. No one is replaceable.

The scariest thing I did was deciding not to go back to corporate America and work for another company. Instead, I decided to go to work for myself. I would take all the success I had earned for others and use that success instead to ensure the future of my son and me.

Sitting here right now, I still can't believe I did it. While I loved the security my steady paycheck provided, I hated the way it made me feel. I wasn't living up to my potential, and I certainly wasn't happy. I was simply surviving—hoping my boss would finally recognize my worth and leave me alone to do what I did best. But that's no way to live.

To find your true calling in life, you need to be willing to take risks and put yourself on the line. This may mean escaping your box by jumping out the window and realizing you've got wings and that they will open when you need them the most. I think we all intuitively know this is the case, but sometimes we have to be pushed out the window to discover our wings have been there all along.

———————

Making the decision to sit alone instead
of sitting at a table where you are not
supported is not easy, but it will be worth it.

———————

There's a little more to the story about that day. When my new boss fired me, she slid two different papers in front of me. One memo simply read: "Heather Monahan has been terminated."

The other memo was much longer, and it said something to the effect of, "Heather Monahan had a wonderful, successful career at the company and sadly has decided to resign and pursue other interests. The company is so supportive and happy for her. We wish her well in her new endeavors, blah, blah, blah."

She also had a stack of papers behind the two memos.

She explained that I could pick whichever memo I wanted to sign. But if I signed the long memo and the stack of papers behind it, she would hand me a check as a parting gift. If I instead decided to sign the one-line memo and leave that stack of papers unsigned, I would get nothing.

After years of countless flights, work trips, leaving my son behind with babysitters, and now being treated terribly by this woman, I knew that she was getting a tremendous amount of pleasure from this final opportunity to twist the knife she had already stabbed deep into my back. I'm certain she was convinced I would sign the longer memo and take the check.

Not today, villain!

I pushed both pieces of paper back across the desk at her and I said, "I didn't write these memos, so I won't be signing either one of them. I'm not sure what you're trying to pull here, but if that is all you've got to say, I'm leaving."

In that moment, the entire dynamic in the room changed.

What the villain didn't know was that I was finally more driven to respect myself than I was to take the money. At that moment, I was no longer the little girl who had grown up poor, without the things the other children in my school had.

I was no longer the young girl who had to put groceries back on the shelf because she didn't have enough money to pay for them.

I was no longer the career woman who always put my company's needs before the needs of myself and my family.

That was a pivotal moment for me—the turning point in my life that sent me down an entirely new path.

As I stood up from that table, I watched as my boss's face turned beet red. She may have won the battle, but she had lost the war. When I stood up for myself that fateful day, I set myself up for finding success and happiness *on my own terms*—not on someone else's. But that success wouldn't come overnight. There was much work to be done. And there was that little thing about not having a paycheck.

As I drove home from the office that last time, I didn't know how I was going to pay the mortgage for my condo, make the payments for my son's school, or take care of all my other bills. But I knew that I had what I needed to figure it out.

That day, that woman thought she had fired me but I had actually just fired my villain. When you fire your villain you set yourself up to take off!

That's what this book is all about. In the pages that follow, I'll reveal to you the lessons I learned after I was fired, and how I used what I learned to rebuild my confidence and find the kind of success that we all dream of having in our lives. I'll show you how to identify the villains in your life and leapfrog right over them—leaving them in your rearview. My goal is to help you wake up excited about the day to come and everything else ahead of you.

Now, let's get started.

CHAPTER 2

Create Confidence in Three Easy Steps

This book is built on the solid foundation of my powerful BAK process, which takes us back to a time in our lives when we were full of happiness, believed in ourselves without question, and were willing to take risks without fear of failure.

You don't think that is true for you? I promise you it is.

As children, we didn't second-guess ourselves before attempting to crawl or walk—we just did it. And if at first we didn't succeed, we picked ourselves up and tried again—and again, and again until we achieved our goal. We embraced the challenge in a fearless and joyful way, full of self-confidence and always optimistic for the future. Take a look at babies learning to crawl or walk. They aren't nervous about what others are thinking. They aren't waiting for someone to give them permission. They have an urge to move and they go all in.

That is where we are going to get you BAK to.

There are three parts to the BAK framework:

Beliefs—the self-talk and other internal messages we have accepted as truth.

Actions—the actions we are currently taking—and plan to take in the future—to find success and happiness.

Knowledge—the information and skills we need to be more effective people in every aspect of our work and personal lives.

Together, BAK will provide you with a powerful and easy-to-implement framework for creating the confidence you need to leapfrog the villains at work, in your career, and in your life.

This book has been designed around the BAK framework—enabling you to quickly and easily identify and read the chapters that focus specifically on whatever it is you need most: working on your self-beliefs, taking action, or expanding your knowledge. I want to give you a sense of what that means in this chapter, and then I need you to jump to the part of the book that resonates most with you. For example, I am an action person. I feel most comfortable with the idea of taking action, so that is the part of the book I would start with. I know plenty of people, however, who are more drawn to self-reflection and would rather start with the belief part. You decide what is right for *you*—there are no wrong answers.

When you start with part I, you are jumping right into examining your own self-talk and inner beliefs. What I have discovered is that for years I had been telling myself a story that was not true. I have a feeling that you, too, have been telling yourself a self-limiting and inaccurate story. Can you think of what that story could be? The one in your head that holds you back from achieving your goals and dreams, time after time? Let's decide today that this story is inaccurate—it's just not true. What would that mean to your life?

Here's an example from my own life: I grew up being called the "social" one while my sister was called the "smart" one. She had perfect grades and flawless SAT scores. She graduated at the top of her class, and she became an accomplished lawyer. I, on the other hand, had always assumed I wasn't smart. Not because anyone called me dumb, but because I saw *her* as the smart one, which I thought meant that I wasn't.

Throughout my life, I told myself the story that I was not smart. That meant that I sat out of meetings if the person coming in had gone to Harvard or some other prestigious university. It meant that I opted out of opportunities in which I could have advanced because I was holding onto the story that I was not intelligent.

Fast-forward to last Christmas when my son, Dylan, and I met my sister and her kids at Walt Disney World. We were sitting talking when my sister shared that she had just taken her kids in for an IQ test. I laughed—who *does* that but my sister?! Of course she had done that, and they are probably geniuses just like her.

She asked me if I had taken Dylan in for the IQ test. I told her no and laughed again. She told me she didn't understand why I didn't get him tested. Then she asked if I had remembered taking the test as a child, and I did not. She told me that the school had directed my mother to bring my sister in for an IQ test. There was no sitter available, so I had to join them. Since I was there, they offered to test me, too, as we were only a year and a half apart in age.

My sister told me that her scores came back off the charts—in the top 1 percent, a genius for sure. Then she also told me that, while my score was not as high as hers, I also rated in the genius range.

Mic drop. This was news to me. I had never heard this story before. I couldn't believe I had spent the previous forty-five years believing I wasn't smart and then behaving in ways that reflected and reinforced this false belief.

Make the decision today to stop telling yourself the story that is holding you back. It just isn't true.

What story are you telling yourself
that is currently holding you back?

If this resonates with you, then jump right to the beliefs part of this book and let's get to work on changing those false beliefs.

Of course, action is my jam. I would always rather do something than self-reflect or evaluate and access knowledge. Maybe because I have loved sports and working out my whole life, or maybe because I understand the power of momentum. If you are like me, you will want to start with part II.

Owning your own voice and speaking up takes practice but with time becomes second nature. Let me give you an example. Twenty years ago, when my confidence was low, I never felt sure if my ideas were good ones. That meant that, if I was in a meeting, I avoided raising my hand for fear that someone else would say mine was a terrible idea. It takes practice, but speaking up can be learned. Speaking up is an action step. Challenging yourself to speak up one time a day and starting off small will work. Baby steps.

I also realize now that people are invited to a meeting or to be on a team because of their potential contributions. By not contributing, you are actually *not* holding up your end of the bargain and *not* warranting your seat at the table. That is a problem.

I have also seen countless times when more experienced people don't speak up or contribute their great ideas because they are afraid those ideas will be seen as antiquated. Conversely, junior people won't share their great ideas for fear that others will say that they don't understand the business or that they missed the mark completely. Both have the potential to add value, but in order to do so, they need to take action and raise their hands. Do your job: speak up and contribute. What is the worst that can happen? Warrant the seat at the table you have been given.

While some people gravitate to beliefs and some to actions, you may be pulled more toward knowledge. If you are most comfortable listening to podcasts or reading books or relying on mentors to learn, then you will want to jump forward to part III. I have learned so much from my time in corporate America, my time in the C-suite, and my time in therapy and studying psychology in college. I am excited to share what I have learned with you.

Here is an example:

Fear is a liar.

This is one of the most powerful statements I have learned in my entire life. Accepting that fear is a liar, nothing but false ideas I have made up in my own mind, has changed everything for me in my life. Some say it's an acronym for False Evidence Appearing Real. Whether it's fear that something could happen to my son, or fear of what could happen to screw up my next presentation, or fear of what someone might say to me, the story created in my mind is *always* worse than any reality.

When I was a kid, I learned that if I felt fear, I should run home and hide. Somehow, I hung on to this concept all through my life. What that did was cripple me in my personal life and in my career. I have since learned that when I feel fear, I should *not* run away and hide. Instead, I should run toward it and embrace it.

Fear is a green light that means go and go faster!

I own the power to dissolve the fear I feel by accepting that it is not real. These days, when I feel fear, I go running right to it. That is the only way to prove it is a liar. And it always pays off for me. It will pay off for you too.

Don't overthink this. Just go to the part of the book that you feel is right for you.

Can't decide? Then just turn the page.

KEY TAKEAWAY

Confidence doesn't have to be elusive. Your confidence is a combination of your beliefs, your actions, and the knowledge you surround yourself with. Pay attention to the beliefs you embrace, the actions you take, and the knowledge you expose yourself to, and you will have everything you need to grow your confidence.

I would love to hear your story and answer your questions!
To continue the conversation, join me wherever you are:

Twitter @_heathermonahan using #BAK
Instagram @heathermonahan using #confidencecreator
Linkedin @theheathermonahan using #overcomeyourvillains

PART I

BELIEFS

CHAPTER 3

Return Others' Self-Limiting Beliefs

"All that we are is the result of what we have thought."

—BUDDHA

While getting fired was the push I needed to overcome the biggest villain in my life—my boss—on the way to finding my true calling, it took me some time to realize that what had happened was actually a good thing and not the complete disaster it felt like at the time.

Driving home from work that fateful day, and for the rest of the week, I cried and wondered what I would do. Since the noncompete clause in my contract prohibited me from taking a similar job in the radio industry, I was cut out of the career I knew and where my value to an employer was. I didn't know what step to take next. What I also didn't know was that my former company would report my company phone as stolen and that Verizon would shut it down, requiring me to get a new phone and new phone number. I know this sounds like a first-world problem, and I get it, but when you are broken, it is devastating. Brushing my hair seemed like a challenge, and getting a new phone number after fourteen years felt inconceivable.

But guess what? It worked out.

I got a new number and the people who really wanted to find me did. The other ones—the ones I thought were my friends but really weren't—didn't bother.

The good news is now I have people who care about me and really do want to be a part of what I have created. They are inspired and excited to be around me. If the people who weren't genuine hadn't ghosted me, I wouldn't have known their true intentions. And I wouldn't be attracting the phenomenal people I have now. Having my phone shut off was hard, but it ended up being a blessing in disguise, just like getting fired. I couldn't see it at first, but a year later I was grateful.

Think of a time in your life when you were scared to do something but moved through the fear and did it anyway. Chances are, you reached your goal, or at least you got a lot closer than you imagined. Use that example as proof that the next goal will work out the same.

Yes, self-doubt will creep back in occasionally, as it does for me. I beat that self-doubt back down with all the crumbs of success I have experienced in the previous week, the previous month, the previous year. I celebrate these small wins and recognize my progress every day. When the old tape starts to run, telling me I can't do something, I switch stations and hit up Kendrick Lamar's "i (Love Myself)," and I remind myself that when you google me, I show up as a keynote speaker, a top-100 podcaster on America's leading podcasting platform, a confidence creator, and an author—not as a radio industry sales executive.

Mind has officially been blown.

What can *you* get done this year if you get rid of others' self-limiting beliefs about who you are, and if you believe in yourself?

What I have realized is I allowed myself to be put in a lane. I was in the "sales" lane, and that was the only lane I was given permission to travel in. If I strayed out of my lane, I was quickly pushed right back in it.

Here's what I have learned: You can smash through all of the lanes—blow them up and get rid of them—and just be you. You can live lanelessly. You can take your unique talents and attributes wherever you want to go. When I blew up the lanes, suddenly there was no more traffic! Get rid of the lanes, create your own space, and things move much more smoothly.

This was an epiphany, and it's absolutely true. Why can't I be Heather who writes books, gives keynotes, and consults for all kinds of businesses? Who said Heather can only be in sales? It really doesn't matter who put me in that lane because I am now crystal clear that it is up to me to go where I want to go and take my unique skills and talents with me. The more I step into who I really am, the stronger and more powerful I become wherever I go.

The same is true for you.

When I finished writing my first, self-published book, *Confidence Creator,* I wanted to share it with my family and my innermost circle before I released it. I told only a few people I was working on the book because I was afraid that people would try to talk me out of doing it. And sure enough, that's exactly what happened.

I was really excited and proud. I was just starting to get comfortable with the idea of smashing through my old sales lane when my brilliant sister called. She had finished speed-reading my manuscript, and I was on high alert, ready for her reaction. It didn't go so well.

She told me immediately that I shouldn't move forward with my book. She explained that, as a lawyer, she needed to advise me not to publish it. She said that I should expect to be sued by my past employers and everyone I called out in the book, even though everything I wrote was true. Not only that, but a well-known author would probably sue me, too, since my manuscript reminded my sister of their book, even though mine was entirely original.

That was it; I was devastated. I thanked my sister for her input, then hung up and cried for hours. I went back under my weighted blanket and struggled, not knowing what to do. Today, it is clear to me that her concerns came from a place of love and wanting to protect me, but I didn't need to take on *her* self-limiting beliefs. I could have simply thanked her for her concerns and kept on going. I wish I had this new 2.0 version of myself then coaching me, but I didn't.

The feedback I really wanted to get was from my mom, but she didn't call. As it turns out, my mom was upset with me. She felt that my book didn't position her in a good light and that the past should remain in the past.

I couldn't believe it. The only person my book didn't position in a good light was me! My book was a compilation of my lowest moments and how I learned to build confidence from them. How could she think that she was the one who would look bad?

I called my father, and he sat in as the mediator so that my mom would listen to me explain that the book was not about her. Yikes, that was painful. I was devastated, and decided I would kill my book.

I sat on my couch crying hysterically. Here I was—I hadn't told anyone I was writing a book, and I was so proud I had done it. I really liked it, but my family members didn't think I should move forward with it, and one of them was a lawyer!

Had I wasted the past few months? Should I just go back to corporate America?

For months I flip-flopped between thinking that I should go to work for myself and thinking I needed to give up my misguided dream and go back to work for someone else. I was torn apart, not sure what to do. What I didn't understand is that I had already jumped and that if I kept second-guessing myself, my wings weren't going to open.

I was sabotaging myself! I remember being young and sabotaging myself, and I can't believe now that month after month after month I was doing it again. Damn, old habits die hard. Which ones are you permitting right now?

In this down moment when I was preparing to scrap my book and start dialing people in my old industry for jobs, I did something *really* smart. I called my editor, Ryan. Ryan had not only written a book, he had written nineteen books. He had way more experience with this than I did. I explained to him what had happened and that I thought I should trash the book.

"Did you write this book for your mom and your sister?" he asked.

"No."

"Did the person you wrote the book for change?"

"No." I had written the book for anyone who struggled with confidence the same way I had for so long. That had not changed.

Ryan continued with his inquisition. "Did you read that other author's book and try to imitate it while you wrote your book?"

"I read her book five years ago," I admitted, "but no—this is my story, not hers."

"Do you think anyone has a copyright on self-help books and that no one else can ever write another one?"

"Nope."

I heard Ryan loud and clear, and I made up my mind. I was going to reject the self-limiting beliefs others were projecting on me and move forward with my book. It was my story, my life, my idea. If they wanted to limit themselves, that was fine, but they would not limit *me*. Ryan had reminded me of my *why*.

When you reconnect with *why* you are doing something, it makes the decision to move forward much easier.

Nothing about this has been easy. Getting the advice of people who have already walked the path I want to take has been a tremendous help for me, and it is something I continue to do to propel myself to the next level. Keep someone on speed dial who is ahead of where you are and tap them when you second-guess yourself or when your inner circle second-guesses you.

You do not have to accept their self-limiting beliefs. You can thank them for offering their perspective and hand it right back. I actually see myself smiling at them and handing it back, and it feels great! So many people believe that they are looking out for you and helping you when they do this, but it is so important that you listen to the one voice that counts: yours.

These days, my inner voice says, "Oh, no thank you. That is not for me, that is for you!" And I move on. Just as you should move on.

I won't leave you hanging. I know what you are thinking. How did things end up with your mother and sister? I am happy to report that both my mother and sister ended up being very supportive of my book after it came out. Sometimes the only way to overcome a hard time is to go through it.

KEY TAKEAWAY

Never take direction from someone who hasn't been where you are attempting to go. Reconnect with your *why*, and move forward with your mission. Leave your self-limiting beliefs in the past—they don't have a place in your future.

Here is a fun exercise I call "flipping the script." Basically, it means choosing to see the opposite of what others may be telling you when they are trying to hold you back. You can choose to see what others are presenting you, or you can choose to reframe it and make it work for you.

I failed and I am done
So don't tell me
I have potential
Because I've realized
I won't get another job
Because I am too old
No one wants someone who was fired
And don't try to tell me
There is a star within me
Because I truly know
I'm unemployable
Nothing you say will get me to believe
I will make a comeback

———

It's time to flip the script
on the naysayers.
You can read from the bottom up,
or I will flip it for you here:

———

I will make a comeback
Nothing you say will get me to believe
I'm unemployable
Because I truly know
There is a star within me
And don't try to tell me
No one wants someone who was fired
Because I'm too old
I won't get another job
Because I've realized
I have potential
So don't tell me
I failed and I am done

Wow! I love this exercise! I am smiling as I flipped the script and read it out loud.

Now, you rewrite it line by line—the way that fits your story best. Then flip the story around and read it out loud. Keep searching for the reframe or the flip the next time someone hands you their self-limiting beliefs. Remember: What someone else believes doesn't have to become your reality. Your beliefs are your choice. Choose wisely.

Thank you, Daniel Abrahams, for the idea!

I would love to hear your story and answer your questions!
To continue the conversation, join me wherever you are:

Twitter @_heathermonahan using #BAK
Instagram @heathermonahan using #confidencecreator
Linkedin @theheathermonahan using #overcomeyourvillains

CHAPTER 4

Make Your Bucket List Real

"Your thoughts become things."

—RHONDA BYRNE

Just like you, I have bucket-list goals, and maybe like you I had not given them a deadline. They had been sitting there on my bucket list—collecting dust. Sure, in theory, they existed, but they weren't part of my daily action plan or conversation, and they definitely weren't materializing. Without action, goals can't become real. If you are ready to move your bucket list from fantasy to reality, then now is the time to set your Google Alerts and get moving.

———

Write down your list of goals.
Put it somewhere visible.
Read it *every* day.

———

A year and a half ago, I was working on my to-do list, which included all sorts of goals I wanted to achieve. I had just accomplished the goal at the top of my list and was ready to get to work on the next one. And there it was, in big letters: TED TALK.

It was time—I got to work.

The first thing I did was to set up a Google Alert for "TEDx" so that anytime an announcement was made—such as Speakers Wanted or Call for Speakers—I would see it in time to apply. It was a great first step toward my TED Talk goal, but here's where I went wrong: I applied to every TEDx opportunity I could find—sending along my speaker reel and pushing what a great speaker I was—assuming it would take only a couple of pitches before someone signed me.

The process went on for a year. Crickets.

During this time, I met Cindy. Cindy is a beautiful woman who attended my book signing at Books and Books in Miami. The night Cindy attended, I also gave a talk.

Afterward, Cindy introduced herself and told me that I should give a TEDx Talk. I was elated! I told her that I desperately wanted to give a TEDx Talk but had been unable to land one. She laughed. What I didn't know was that Cindy was on the local TEDx team in Boca Raton. And while her 2018 event had just taken place, Cindy said she would explain to me how to land a talk.

A couple of months later, when I was becoming increasingly frustrated with my inability to secure a talk, Cindy set aside some time to discuss my approach with me. Here's what she taught me: You are going about this all wrong. TEDx people are all volunteers—they are busy people who love TEDx and who love big ideas. Figure out what the theme is for the event (every TEDx event establishes a theme in advance) and come up with a Big Idea that ties into their theme. The *idea* is the key, not *you*. (Mic drop.)

Next, cater to the TEDx team and provide them with whatever it is they need to decide in your favor. Remember that they are the ultimate decision makers. They receive a constant stream of hundreds, if not thousands, of applications all year round, and you need to find a way to stand out.

When you are trying to convince
someone to do something,
make it about *them*, not *you*.

Cindy's advice was fantastic, and I immediately changed my approach.

More crickets.

So, I took my TED Talk goal down a notch on my priority list—moving it to the back burner—and put the focus on my new Podcast. I had plenty of work to do to get that set up.

One day, I saw Cindy post on LinkedIn, and I tried reaching out to her again. While we were chatting, I asked her if there was any way I could take the stage with my big idea at TEDxBocaRaton since it was still months away. She said that I should apply, and she would offer any feedback she could. Great!

I applied. Cindy got my application, reviewed it, and let me know she thought my idea was a good one. I felt hopeful!

The theme of her TEDx event was "Rethinking Relationships." My idea worth sharing was that students with mediocre grades shouldn't be looked down upon—instead, mediocrity in school could be an indicator that the child may be destined for leadership success. My talk would be titled "C-Student to the C-Suite." I would ask everyone in the audience to rethink the relationship we have with grades and what they tell us as a child. And, since I had been an average student and made it to the C-suite, I was certain I would be the perfect person to dive into the topic.

After two months, many phone calls, a tall stack of thank-you notes, and a lot of pleading, I was officially notified that I had been selected for TEDxBocaRaton. Yay! I immediately sat down to begin drafting my talk.

The TEDx team provided fantastic direction by way of two videos that detailed what makes a good TED Talk and why. With that direction, I was on my way. I quickly knocked out a script, tailoring it to the eighteen-minute window I assumed everyone got. The announcement was made that I would be a speaker and I was overjoyed! I had finished writing my talk, checked it off my to-do list, and was on to the next priority.

Until I wasn't.

A month later, I received a call from Cindy. The TEDxBocaRaton team had decided that my big idea wasn't quite big enough. I would need to scrap it and start over. Fortunately, Cindy was willing to help.

She stayed on the phone with me and we brainstormed new, bigger ideas. We went back and forth for a week on different concepts and agreed on a new idea: rethinking the relationship between women in the workplace. This quickly morphed into my big idea TED Talk: "The Me Too Movement: Misstep or Mistake?"

Wow. This was a bold move and one that I personally felt comfortable delivering. But every time I shared the concept with someone, they were shocked and told me how ballsy I was taking this on. They told me that I would upset people and should rethink if I really wanted to do this.

Never take direction from someone who hasn't been where you are going.

I felt fine with the concept, the idea, and my truth in the idea, so I moved ahead, thanking my friends and colleagues for their feedback.

I didn't think much about the talk again for the next month or so—everything was on track. The head of TEDxBocaRaton liked my idea, and his speaker coach thought it was great too. The timeline they provided for all of the speakers was very detailed. It included coaching calls you are expected to complete, as well as Zoom video calls with the head of the TEDx event. There were dates to do a walk-through, other dates for sponsor events, and yet other dates for VIP events and more. There were a lot of dates, and I was surprised how much went into putting this together. This was not like giving a regular keynote where you show up, give your speech, and go home. This is a TED Talk, and the many requirements and restrictions made it feel different.

Exactly two months before the event, I received an email from the team. I would be allotted ten minutes for my talk.

What?!

What happened to the eighteen minutes I was supposed to get? Here's the thing with speaking: the longer the speech, the easier it is. As Woodrow Wilson once said, "If I am to speak ten minutes, I need a week for preparation; fifteen minutes, three days; if half an hour, two days; if an hour, I am ready now." Needless to say, I needed to rework my talk from top to bottom, then start preparing to give it.

We cannot expect things to always go our way. The more we embrace the unexpected, the faster we can pivot.

Before I knew it, the day for walk-throughs arrived, and I was feeling really excited to go. As soon as I got into the car, I started preparing what I was going to say. The words just came to me and it was the craziest thing! I arrived at the venue—there had been a fire the night before, but I was assured that everything was fine. I took the stage, walked around, and felt fantastic. On the ride back to Miami, the words just flowed. I ran into my house, sat down, and typed everything out. I had googled how many words a speech should be to hit ten minutes, and I was within the range. This was working out fabulously!

Next, I sent my proposed talk to the speaker coach, the organizer, and to my friend Amy Morin, who has a successful TEDx talk with over 14 million views. I had saved my talk under the title "TedTalk-50MViews." I was going big or going home.

I heard back good news from everyone except the speaker coach and my friend Amy.

The coach didn't like my intro, and she also didn't like that I didn't talk more about what happened to me after I got fired. I didn't agree with her, so I didn't care. I listened to my intuition over others' advice. I thanked her for her feedback and moved on.

My friend Amy sent me the most amazing and encouraging email, but she challenged me to find a better intro, too — something that was relevant to my topic yet would still pull the viewer in. Yikes! I thought my intro was great, but both Amy and the speaker coach said I needed to step it up. I knew I had to think about it.

To make her advice more palatable, Amy used the "sandwich technique." The sandwich technique puts a piece of constructive criticism between two slices of praise. Amy led off by talking about what she loved about my talk, then she mentioned what she thought I could improve, and then she closed by saying she knew I would kill it and deliver an amazing talk. I've got to admit that her approach worked.

It wasn't just her approach that won me over though. Amy had already been where I wanted to go, so she had proven her credibility, which was key to me. I was convinced I should take her advice.

It was twelve days before my first TEDx event, and I was beginning to think I really needed some outside help. I wanted to at least get the chance to give my talk in front of someone other than my reflection in the mirror. That's when I decided to call a different speaker coach, Natalie, who had coached my son when he needed to give a big speech at school the year before and was running into some challenges. I loved Natalie's energy and vibe and excitement, and I knew she was the perfect person for me to speak in front of. She had secured a mini-venue for the occasion, and I stood up — notes in hand — to give my talk.

The decision to bring in Natalie turned out to be a great one. Not only did she encourage me and give me some specific tips—such as using my fingers to highlight each of my five main points and count them out—she also opened my mind to something that I wasn't seeing, and it was powerful.

Natalie knew that I am not against the Me Too movement, and that my talk was about taking it to the next level. She wondered, however, if other people would realize that too. She wanted to make sure that they did, so she explained the concept of "Yes, and . . ." to me.

Yes, and . . . is a technique used in improvisational comedy. Instead of having to pick something—like you can have this or that—you expand the thought to include more options. I completely understood what she was saying, and I made sure to highlight that I am a Me Too movement supporter, and I want to expand Me Too to include the sneaky villain a woman doesn't expect.

Yes, and . . .

Land mine avoided.

Natalie also pointed out things that I had done well in my movement onstage, so I locked in on the strong points and used them as anchors in my mind. She recorded my talk, and when I tell you I had just come from the gym with no makeup on and dirty hair in a knot, you can guess it was not my finest moment. But getting to watch those videos at home helped immensely. I saw what I liked and what I didn't like, and I got a new perspective on myself.

Identifying anchors when you make
a presentation is key to nailing
your powerful moments.

We had discussed my opening and Natalie liked it, so I didn't change it though I still wondered if maybe I should.

The next few days were busy, and I had completely forgotten that Kristina, one of my best friends from home, was coming into town. She had rented a house in the Keys Wednesday through Sunday, and my son, Dylan, and I were going to stay with them Thursday through Sunday. Probably not the best time to go on vacation considering I was just one week out from my TEDx presentation, but we had committed, and we were going to follow through.

I'm so glad we went. We stayed in the most beautiful area I had never been to before. And I actually got some work done. When I went for a run, I would give my talk in my mind, which triggered some great new lines to try out. Also, I found my dream vacation house, and I ran to it each morning—envisioning my TED Talk going viral and all of the books I would sell and how I would buy this amazing new home.

Saturday turned out to be a bit gloomy, so Dylan; my friend's daughter, Sasha; and I went for a walk. We found a real estate advertising magazine during our travels, and we all climbed into my SUV and set out to go house-hunting. Dylan pretended he was the local real estate agent we had met, and Sasha laughed hysterically in the back seat. All day we drove around Ocean Reef, marking up our real estate magazine and pulling in to look at homes ranging from $4 million to $22 million.

As you might expect given the price range, these homes were exceptional. Massive and sprawling and nearly every single one on the ocean. Dylan and I live on the water but in a high-rise. We have both been dreaming of moving to a nice, single-family home on the water, and suddenly, it was beginning to feel like our dream would come true. Just 50 million views of my TED Talk and we could afford this home. I could see it clear as day, and it didn't seem like a dream at all.

That night at dinner, I shared with Kristina that I needed to work on my talk. I was seven days away from *go* time and still didn't know about the intro. Kris and the kids lined up and listened as I paced the living room and gave my talk. The next day, she suggested a new intro, and as it turned out, I loved it! She told me that after listening to my talk, she went to bed that night, and the idea just came to her the next day. I wrote up the changes, and Dylan and I headed home with less than a week to go. After Dylan went to bed, I practiced my talk late into the night.

I went to a media event on Tuesday, and I asked the audience if they would indulge me by letting me do a test run of my ten-minute TEDx presentation. They were excited to hear it, so I got started. I stopped just once when I forgot a line, but I finished strong. I hit the ten-minute mark almost perfectly, and the audience went wild. I was feeling a *lot* better!

I had never prepared so much for a talk in my life. I knew this was a rare opportunity—my number one goal—and I was going to make the most of it. I had even taken the top ten strongest statements from my talk and written them on large pieces of paper I stuck all over the walls of my condo. Dylan just rolled his eyes. I had to laugh! It was a bit crazy, but I am a very visual person and I like to see things—it helps me. I had decided not to memorize my talk word for word because I didn't want it to seem canned. One thing Kindra Hall revealed on my podcast was that she lost a speaking contest because she was too prepared and too perfect. That definitely made good sense. I would rather be my imperfect self so others could relate to me versus being so perfect—and so fake.

Never run away from what
makes you different.

Little did I know just how far from perfect I actually was—that revelation was still a few days away.

The next day, I flew to New York City to give a speech at the Guggenheim Museum. During the flight, I read and reread my TEDx presentation—taking notes to remind myself where I wanted to speak slower to emphasize a point, or where I could pick up the pace to share a story. After I landed, I made a quick stop at my hotel, then wheeled into the museum and said hello to everyone. My friend Scott introduced me to the group, and I started my speech. I began by explaining how Scott and I had become friends and why my book was so important to me. Suddenly, out of the corner of my eye, I saw a woman pass out. She fell into the woman standing next to her, who fell into the next person, and so on. It was like a long line of dominoes all falling down in sequence until the entire table behind them had smashed to the ground with glass breaking everywhere. To say it was instant chaos would be an understatement.

There was no ignoring this, so I quickly said, "Well, it appears that someone over here knows I am giving my first TEDx presentation this Saturday. And, as you know with TED Talks, they say that anything and everything can and will go wrong. So I would just like to thank whoever it was that decided to stir things up tonight. I am grateful to you."

Then I moved to the heart of my speech, and it was very well received. I had decided to build my talk around a five-step approach I used in my previous role as a C-suite media executive to build winning advertising campaigns. Why not use this same approach to create an ad campaign for me, by me, to elicit confidence within me? So, after my introduction, I launched into the five steps anyone could use to build their own confidence:

1. Identify your platform to run your campaign.
2. Include a visual component to the campaign to get explosive results.
3. Choose powerful messaging and run it with frequency.
4. Select a jingle to elicit emotion and memory.
5. Add a call to action to convert the opportunity.

Before the night wrapped and I headed back to my hotel room, a gentleman I had never met gave me a wonderful bit of advice. He shared that the most important thing when giving a TED Talk is that I be *me*. No matter what, bring the real me to the talk and it would be great. There's a reason why I wrote a note to myself that I see every day: *Just Be You!* I flew home the next day—working on my talk during the return flight. I wasn't done yet, though. After I landed, I went home to shower and get ready for the VIP sponsor event in Boca Raton.

Just be *you*!

I found it perplexing that we would have a mandatory party to attend the night before the TEDx event, but I wasn't complaining, so I went on my way. I practiced my talk again in the car, and when I arrived at the party venue, I talked and took photos with our sponsors and chatted up anyone and everyone. I wanted to make sure I did a good job, knowing how hard all of the volunteers had worked.

At 9:30 p.m., I asked if I could go home since I had such a long ride back to Miami. For two months straight, the only television I had been watching was TED Talks. I knew that watching these talks would help make me feel at home on the TEDxBocaRaton stage. That night was no different, even though it was getting late. I fell asleep at midnight—watching the top TED Talks—and woke up early the next morning and got ready for our TEDx team meeting.

The car ride to Boca was great—I was listening to the playlist that fires me up like nothing else. I was *on fire*. I walked into the venue in my sweats with my eye patches, and Erik told me I would speak first. How exciting! I was stoked. He told me to stay with him onstage as they wanted to mic me and do a few minutes of my talk. The other speakers were with Ron—walking backstage and discussing the flow of the day and what to expect. After my mic was in place, Erik asked me to walk onto the stage and give my talk—he would cut me off when he had enough.

I took that stage like a boss and I started my talk like a million bucks!

But then, a few minutes in, something happened. My mind went blank. Not just a little bit—completely, utterly, *blank*.

I was frozen and flustered and getting a little frantic.

Erik laughed and said as if it wasn't a big deal, "Oh, Heather forgot a line, but I got enough—we are good. Thanks, Heather."

No one seemed to care but me. I was *mortified*. When I stepped off the stage, it was as if I was in a fog. Then, a woman next to me said, "I have a friend like you. It was his biggest game in the NFL, and he missed the field goal kick. The kick he had done a million times, and this was the moment that counted, and he missed it."

I was livid. The only words that came to mind were, "Wow, thanks, but that's not very helpful right now. I need to go."

I told Erik I needed to leave to get ready, and I headed to the hotel. I was shaking and panicked. What if I froze when I was out there onstage for real?

I got to the hotel and my hair god, Jacob, and my makeup artist, Cynthia—who both know me well—saw my Category 5 emergency and jumped right on it. I sat down and I started giving my talk—five times in a row. They were cheering me on and telling me how amazing it was. I was still a mess inside, but at least now I looked good. Cynthia and I beelined back to the event because it was almost go time. We went back to the speaker area, and it was packed with sponsors and people wanting to speak with me. But my mind wasn't in the room. All I wanted to do right then was find a safe space where I could be alone to practice my talk with my music playing. It wasn't to be.

So I did the next best thing.

I put my earbuds in and launched my playlist—seeing myself take the stage like a boss in my mind. I had to tune out everyone and everything around me. Finally, Cynthia and I were taken backstage and I was told I was on in five minutes. Frantic people were every-where—the backstage area was filled with speakers who were in panic mode, pacing and practicing, or other people who wanted to talk to me. I found a kitchen that didn't have many people where Cynthia and I could sit and talk and listen to my music before I went onstage.

We were walked over to the stage, and a nice girl handed me some lavender essential oil. All I can say is, lavender for the save!

I have used lavender to calm me down for years; however, this moment it was literally saving my life. I inhaled the lavender oil, then passed it to the man who was scheduled to speak right after me—he was a complete and nervous wreck. I breathed deeply and looked at my notes one last time. Cynthia told me I was going to be great.

I believed her.

In the short moment as I walked onto the stage to begin my TEDx presentation, I said to myself, "If you go out there and bomb, it doesn't matter. I will always be proud of you for going. And if you don't go out there, you will never forgive yourself. F this—I'm going!"

I walked out from behind the curtain and headed for the red dot on the stage—my mark—not knowing what was going to happen next. But I turned my fate over to something so much bigger than me, in hopes that everything would be okay.

And it was. In fact, it was better than okay—*much* better.

They say that the talk owns you, or you own the talk.

This time, I *owned* the talk.

But what I really did was just believe I could.

KEY TAKEAWAY

A priority to us may not be a priority to others. They will have their own priorities, so we need to move forward to advance our initiatives through other avenues yet be ready to circle back to those same people for help as their priorities change. Timing is everything, and just because timing doesn't work the first time doesn't mean that it won't in the future.

I can't wait to hear what you think!
My TEDx Talk has been promoted by TED and
translated into six languages.
Here's a link to my ten-minute TEDx Talk:
https://youtu.be/rZtAJxvgGYw.
Share with me your thoughts wherever you are:

Twitter @_heathermonahan using #BAK
Instagram @heathermonahan using #confidencecreator
Linkedin @theheathermonahan using #overcomeyourvillains

CHAPTER 5

Take Others Off the Pedestal and Level Your Playing Field

"Your beliefs pave your way to success or block you."

—MARSHA SINETAR

Have you ever looked at others and imagined that their lives are perfect, that they don't have any problems? Have you thought they were better than you? Smarter than you? Different in a way you can't compare to? Do you realize, every time you do that, you are holding them to an unrealistic standard and putting yourself down?

When you put others up on a pedestal,
you put yourself beneath them.

The flight home from LA had Wi-Fi and I was checking my direct messages on social media. I had discovered that one of the ways to get rave reviews for my book was to personally respond to every DM. This was time-consuming, but it had a very positive effect on sales. So often, people think you are killing it when, in reality, you are dying to break through all of the noise out there. Every review and rating on Amazon and Audible was pure gold—building my credibility as a self-published, first-time author.

I was reading through the DMs when I almost fell out of my seat.

My eyes were glued to a DM from an NBA player. He said that he had read my book and that confidence was a huge thing for him as a professional basketball player. Not only that, but he wanted to speak with me about my book.

What?

Okay, this was beyond comprehension to me. First thing, I was going to make sure I wasn't getting punked—it wouldn't be the first time. I dug into his profile, googled him, and confirmed the DM was real. Knowing that everyone struggles with confidence is one thing, but then seeing it materialize from real people—and, now, a professional athlete—blew me away. I couldn't believe this was happening.

The next day, I got a call from his agent.

He explained that this talented player was beyond exceptional and ready to go to the next level; however, there had been some recent challenges in his life. Injuries and personal situations had hit his confidence pretty hard, and he was getting nervous as the season was almost ready to kick off. He asked if I would meet with them.

I panicked. I was spouting out crazy things like, "I can't—I am so swamped," and "There's no time—I'm heading to New York in the morning!"

The agent laughed. He said, "Great! We will be in New York, too—we will come to you!"

When we feel intimidated,
we want to hide.
This is *never* the answer.

This could not be happening. Yes, I had written a book about my low moments and how I learned to create confidence, but I didn't know anything about coaching an NBA player who makes millions of dollars a year. I felt like a fraud. I also felt that if they met with me and I couldn't help him, I would be exposed as a fraud—an imposter.

I was not in the best of spirits on my flight to New York—I was so stressed out. The crazy thing is that I was heading there for a book launch party put on by my friend Scott. I had met Scott the year before through LinkedIn when my ex-fiancé's daughter was considering going to NYU. I saw that Scott had connections there, and I sent him a DM asking if he could speak to her. He was very generous and arranged to have another student talk with her and answer her questions.

About a month later, he reached out to me to ask if I would contribute a chapter to his upcoming book, *Standing O!* The book was for charity and included some amazing authors, athletes, entrepreneurs, and CEOs. I was so busy trying to get my own book off the ground that, at first, I didn't see how I would be able to make the time. Then I remembered how Scott had made time for me when I needed his help, so I knew I needed to show up for him now.

But I still struggled with the idea that someone would find anything I wrote to be of value. I wondered how long it would feel this way. When would I begin to get comfortable in this new world? Why was it so hard for me to embrace this change and let go of the past? These were questions I would ask myself a lot.

As I worried about the future and about how to build a new kind of career, I would go back and forth in my mind. Should I just go back to the security of a job in media doing the same thing I used to? In so many ways, that path looked like the best choice. I knew where it would lead to, and I knew how to get where I wanted to go. I already had the roadmap.

The new path I was on was not at all clear for me. There was no map for me to follow. I had no idea exactly where I was going from day to day. This new road wasn't clear, and it was full of surprises— not all good, and many scary.

This was so challenging.

I landed in New York and went straight to the same Marriott I always stayed in. I am such a creature of habit, and staying in the same places and being with people I trust always makes me feel better. My good friend George was there. I was so happy to see him—it took my mind off of this crazy experience.

As usual, what I wear really impacts how confident I feel. I had a knee-length white dress with me to wear to the book launch event that evening, but I didn't think it was the best outfit to meet the NBA player and his agent in the hotel bar beforehand. I decided I would feel more myself in workout pants and a zip-up, so that's what I decided to wear.

Whenever I am getting ready to walk into a situation I feel nervous about, I remind myself of other times I felt the same way and made it back alive. That always makes me smile. I also use the same playlist. It puts me in a mindset that reminds me what it feels like walking into a situation not knowing what's going to happen but setting myself up for something really good. I started envisioning myself going to the meeting, the meeting going really well, and then having a successful book launch party.

I had the NBA player really high up on the proverbial pedestal. I took out the lavender handwipes I keep in case of emergency and inhaled the fragrance in hopes it would calm me down. It did. Then I bombed a chardonnay and forced myself out the hotel room door.

I knew if I tried to peek downstairs, I would end up not going to the meeting. So I stayed focused on just one thing: walking to the elevator and getting on. Once the doors closed behind me, I was trapped. The elevator was taking me right to the eighth floor where the doors would open to the hotel bar.

Deep breath.

I said to myself, "You wrote this book *Confidence Creator,* and you can at least share some of the ways you create confidence. You can do this!"

———

Choose to be your biggest cheerleader!
If you don't believe
wholeheartedly in yourself,
why would anyone else?

———

I kept repeating these words in my mind the entire elevator ride. Then, right before I got off the elevator, I told myself, "I love you; you got this!" I knew if I approached these two men standing tall and strong with a big smile, my confidence would rise to the occasion. So that's exactly what I did.

Taking a quick look around the bar area, it was immediately clear who I was meeting with. The NBA player and his agent had a table roped off in an area away from the other guests. They were also the tallest people in the room by at least a foot—maybe more. I smiled and walked toward them. I saw the NBA player clutching my book. And as I got closer to him, I started to see things differently.

He was clutching my book hoping it could help him—and hoping I could too.

In that moment I saw my eleven-year-old son hanging onto me. That shift allowed me to feel so much better because, all of a sudden, I knew I could help this accomplished man in some way—even if it was just that I showed up to show him he is worth it. That alone would create confidence in him. I smiled *really* big!

———

Sometimes our mind plays tricks on us,
and we need to show up to
see the real situation.

———

He was so excited to meet me, and he asked me to sign his book. I felt so special and so happy. The three of us talked for fifteen minutes and then his agent left. That's when the NBA player started to share what had hit his confidence so hard.

Everyone has different triggers, and everyone has a unique story. For some people, health scares throw them for a loop, while for others, getting into a rut starts a self-destructive path to nowhere. I listened to him—*really* listened to him—as he shared his story. There was one thing that really stuck out to me. He had been dating a woman for a while and she did not sound nice at all. He explained some of the things she had done, and I gave him a look. A look that says, "She did *what?*"

He laughed and told me that he knew what I was saying—that he was just too nice.

Now wait a minute.

There's something worth noting here, because I have heard it from men and women alike: being taken advantage of is never to be confused with being too nice. In fact, how could anyone ever be *too* nice? Being too nice simply means you are a sweet person who is being taken advantage of.

The most important person for you to be nice to is *you*.

I explained to him that this woman was his villain and didn't deserve to be around him or with him or drive his car or live at his house. She was taking advantage, and that is grounds for termination.

He laughed and shared that he had just broken up with her and was already feeling much better. We sat, and he shared his story with me for hours. It really felt as if I were sitting with my son ten years from now. Life teaches you lessons—good and bad—and, if you don't have a close mentor to help guide you through those times, things can get tough and seem confusing or muddy. Steering this man back to good people, to listening to his own inner voice, and to doing what felt good for him would make him confident again.

We had been talking for two hours when I suddenly realized I was going to be late for the book launch!

I let him know that I was really late and needed to go. Before I left, the player shared one more issue with me. He told me that when he is on the free-throw line in a game, he becomes incredibly nervous and doesn't do well. But when he is in practice, he nails every shot.

I started laughing, but he didn't find my laughter funny at all. He told me I didn't get it because I wasn't a professional athlete and didn't know what it was like being the center of attention for everyone to stare at. But that's what I found so funny!

I told the player that when I first started speaking years earlier, I felt exactly the same way—like I was at the center of attention for everyone to stare at. But as I gained experience, I started realizing it wasn't that everyone was focused on me—far from it. Half of the audience was playing with their phones, or thinking about dinner, or doing all sorts of things besides focusing on me. The challenge with speaking was to get them *to* focus on me so that they would hear me and listen to what I had to say.

That was the hardest part.

I let the NBA player know that I had been to his games before and had seen him play. I couldn't remember one way or the other if he hit his free throws because I was either texting or in the bathroom or talking to my son about what he wanted to eat. The reality is that people are always more concerned and focused on themselves, and that frees us up to the truth that we are the only ones who are so laser focused on *us*.

"Let the pressure go," I told him. "It wasn't real to begin with."

With that, we hugged, and I ran back upstairs to change into my dress and dart to the book launch party. I thankfully made it well before the party ended. It was a beautiful event, and the support I received from everyone was so amazing.

It was just one more reminder to me that making time to help others always pays off in the end.

Always.

KEY TAKEAWAY

Putting others on a pedestal simply puts us beneath them. Making the decision that we are all equal puts us on the same footing as everyone else. Equal ground, equal opportunity.

I would love to hear your story and answer your questions!
To continue the conversation, join me wherever you are:

Twitter @_heathermonahan using #BAK
Instagram @heathermonahan using #confidencecreator
Linkedin @theheathermonahan using #overcomeyourvillains

CHAPTER 6

Get Empowered by Seeing Your Value Through Others' Eyes

"The only limits you have are the limits you believe."

—WAYNE DYER

Some events in life are unexpected. When I act on something, there is always a chance for a domino effect with all sorts of unintended consequences—some good, and some not so great.

This Thanksgiving was no different.

I sent out an email blast to my entire LinkedIn community, which at the time included in the neighborhood of twenty thousand people. I was offering copies of my first book at a special price since it was a day of gratitude and I wanted to show my gratitude for all the people who had supported me. What I hadn't expected was that Dr. Richard Siegel would respond to me directly.

Dr. Siegel is someone I had worked with years before when I was trying to come to terms with my past and process the abuse I had experienced growing up —more on that to come. He was great to work with. He used a variety of unconventional methods, such as envisioning things. For example, if I told him that I felt disgusting, he might suggest that I take that feeling along with all of my clothes and even that old house and throw it into a giant washing machine. Then he would work with me to envision it as if it were real. I would feel the entire house being washed and everything being cleaned free of that awful past.

Probably sounds a little odd, but bottom line is it worked! To me, Dr. Siegel was an expert in psychology, and I put him on a pedestal.

I got the email from Dr. S. the day after Thanksgiving. It said something like, "Heather, I am so proud of you and what you have created. I would love to collaborate on an event or something where we can help people."

I was floored. Blown away. A doctor wanted to collaborate with me!

I was beyond excited, but I started to feel my fear creep in. I was no doctor, and I felt a little intimidated. We messaged back and forth for a bit and finally got on a call, but neither of us was sure what it was we would do together. Should we host an in-person workshop? Should we create an online event? Should we join an existing event to test our collaboration? There were far too many questions, so I offered up the easiest thing I could think of, Facebook Live. I figured we could test the concept there and see if it worked.

That was the easy part. Now, who was going to do what?

Dr. S. had expertise in medicine, and I had expertise in sales and marketing, so it was beginning to look like I would handle putting this together and he would join me at the live event.

Time passed, and I wasn't doing anything to move things forward—it was painfully obvious. Why wasn't I taking action?

I started to notice I was feeling a bit intimidated. While I was excited to elevate myself and my credibility by partnering with a well-known doctor, I was also feeling intimidated to deliver at a higher level, and that felt scary.

I decided to reverse-engineer the event. If I was stuck and I wasn't taking action, then I would go to social media and announce the event and the day and time. Announcing the event online was just the pressure I needed to make myself move—and move quickly.

When you feel stuck, take the leap
to hold yourself accountable.
Successful people don't always
know the *how*; they trust themselves to
figure it out along the way.

Dr. S. never used social media, so I had to talk to him about setting up a profile so he would be able to join the live event. I sent him a few articles about live online events so he would know what he was walking into. Yes, he has forty-plus years of practice working with patients, but I was able to help him show up for this event. He was super appreciative that I promoted the event and helped him navigate Facebook. That was easy for me.

Keep in mind that just because something is easy for you, that doesn't mean it's easy for others. That is where your value lies. Dr. S. saw value in what I was doing for the event because *he* was doing something new—something he had never done before.

The night before our event we did a live call so I could walk him through setup and answer any questions he might have. This time *I* was the expert. I had done so many Facebook Lives by that time that I felt at ease, but he did not. He asked, "What if I cough a lot?"

"No problem. I will jump in and talk until you feel better."

"But what if this doesn't resonate with a large group and only works one-on-one?"

That's when I knew he was feeling a little bit nervous, just like I get when I am going for something new and putting myself out of my comfort zone. So I jumped right in and gave him some of the amazing feedback I had already heard about people who were excited to learn from him. I explained that I would handle any challenges that arose, and we had nothing to worry about. While this was new for him, it was routine for me.

I finally realized the value I brought to our partnership, and I was feeling good about moving forward.

At the end of our call, Dr. S. said, "I think we should say one last thing at the end: 'Heather and I may be working on a tentative event in the future so reach out if you are interested.'"

I broke out in a huge smile. Of course, I would be honored to hold an event with Dr. S. and help more people. But I told him that we should announce our next event like this: "'Heather and I are holding an upcoming workshop, and if you are ready to go to the next level, message Heather directly so you can be put on the list for this exclusive event.'"

Boom.

Yes, Dr. S. is bringing value, and yes, I am too. I know now that roles don't need to remain one way forever. I have learned that there are moments when I am the mentor, and moments later, I can be the mentee. It's not about age, it's about the different roles and experience we all have. Both roles are okay, and all of us need to step into them. I learn this time and again as I show up as the real me.

Imagine where *you* could be adding value if you put yourself out there. The possibilities are truly endless, and they are limited only by *you*. Choosing to believe it is possible is where you should begin right now.

KEY TAKEAWAY

We may look at others through rose-colored glasses at times. It's important to realize that others may look at us through those same lenses. Although you might not know it yet, you may be able to add value or teach someone how to do something. The only way you'll find out is to show up and ask.

I would love to hear your story and answer your questions!
To continue the conversation, join me wherever you are:

Twitter @_heathermonahan using #BAK
Instagram @heathermonahan using #confidencecreator
Linkedin @theheathermonahan using #overcomeyourvillains

CHAPTER 7

Find Certainty Within

"If you think you can, you can.
If you think you can't, you can't."

—DEL HOWARD

March 5, 2020, was my last live speaking engagement.

I had the opportunity to speak at an international finance conference, and I was nervous. I had never spoken at a finance conference before, and this was my first time addressing an international audience. Double whammy. Because I have learned to trust myself, however, I knew I would find a common thread to join me with the audience.

The day before I was going to speak, I racked my brain—hoping to find a way to connect with them. That's when I remembered that my ex-husband had worked in the finance industry. And while I had not been in the industry myself, I *did* have an insider's peek into how competitive it was, and I could empathize with their challenges.

So I decided to open with that story to relate and connect with them. And it was a hit!

Anytime we can find a common
thread between ourselves and others, we
develop connection and
relatability that is powerful.

After the event, I went to the cocktail party. This was my first speaking engagement for a new speakers bureau, and I wanted the feedback to be off the charts. I worked the room, shaking everyone's hands (I had no idea that just one week later, COVID-19—which had been in the news—would make this simple gesture taboo) and asking for feedback. The feedback was fantastic. I was so proud! I had stepped into the unknown again and it had paid off!

It is amazing how fast things can
change in our world and how
incredibly unexpected it can be.
That's why we always need to
get up, dress up, and show up.

Then, on March 7, I received the email from my literary agent that she had accepted the fifteenth version of my book proposal. Yes, that means that on my *fifteenth* rewrite it was finally a go.

I don't want to downplay this.

For one full year, I had worked hard to first land my agent, then write and rewrite my book proposal—all in the hopes that one day I would be able to get a publisher to say yes. But I've got to admit there were times near the end of this yearlong process that I became frustrated and started second-guessing whether I had targeted the right agent and if I was a good enough writer for the "big leagues."

I can still clearly remember my agent's feedback on the fourteenth version of my proposal. While she saw major improvement, she still knew I could do better.

I was frustrated!

So much so that I had secretly decided that if version number fifteen wasn't the charm, then I was going to move on to find someone else who I hoped would believe in me 100 percent. There was no science behind this decision. I had no experience writing book proposals, and this was the first time I had worked with a literary agent. I knew only that I had been told *no* fourteen times when I thought the proposal—especially the latest version, which I thought was fantastic—should have gotten me a *yes*.

This doesn't mean that I thought this agent was a villain; she was definitely not that. It simply meant I was wondering if I would ever be the right fit for her, and her for me. The fact that this was my first time working with her and my first time working on a book proposal put me in some very unfamiliar territory. I was uncomfortable, confused, and not sure where to turn next. I was questioning *everything*, including myself.

I reluctantly revised the proposal one more time, sent it to my agent, and waited.

Out of the blue, I got a *yes*!

Just like that, my reality changed completely. I had no idea that version fifteen would be the charm, and now I can see that my agent believed in me completely. As she told me, she knew the proposal could be better, and she was right! Just remember that, if I had thrown in the towel at version fourteen, you wouldn't be reading this today. Success often looks easy from the outside, but on the inside, it can be a real test to your self-confidence. It's all about getting knocked down fourteen times, then picking yourself back up fifteen times.

Don't give up too soon on you!

As all this was going on, we were entering a global pandemic. I was so excited to get a *yes* from my agent that I didn't think about anything else but celebration! The next step was for my agent to send a letter to her target list of ideal publishers, describing who I was, what my new book was about, and asking if they wanted a copy of the proposal to review. She sent out fifteen letters, and we waited.

The following week, as the virus began to spread across the US, we began to receive feedback from publishers. Some of the feedback was positive, and some negative, but we did have several publishers that were interested—and even one that was *very* interested. My agent sent out the fifteenth version of my proposal to the interested publishers, and we waited as the virus continued to spread.

One of the ways I relieve stress is to take action. Sometimes that can mean going for a workout, other times that means preparing for the worst. I had ordered water, protein shakes, canned foods, paper towels, toilet paper, and the bare necessities for survival.

Before taking action, however, I always ask myself, "What's the grief-to-gross ratio for this action?" In other words, what's the work put in versus the potential outcome? If the potential outcome is greater than the amount of work required to make it happen, then I will move ahead. Conversely, if the amount of work going into it outweighs the potential outcome, then it is time to reevaluate.

When deciding if I should act
on something, I ask:
What's the grief-to-gross ratio?

Next thing I knew, I received my first *no* from a publisher. Then another and another. Given the timing of this feedback—at the same time I was in quarantine with my son, with all of my speaking engagements canceled (my number one revenue stream)—I was beyond down. I jumped on the phone with one of my good friends to vent about my current situation when I was reminded:

It's not how many *no*s you get.
The truth is, you only need one *yes*!

That shifted my focus immediately. Yes, I had received four *no*s, but my agent had sent out fifteen pitches, and I needed only one of them to come back a *yes*. I was suddenly feeling optimistic. This reminded me of playing softball when I was a kid. As a pitcher, when I would throw three balls, instead of worrying that I was about to walk the batter, I would celebrate that now I only needed to throw three strikes to get that batter out. It's all in how you view the opportunity in front of you.

During this time, my son's school was moved to a virtual classroom at home via his computer and Zoom technology. The transition went okay, although the first week was definitely an adjustment. Becoming my son's Zoom school lunch lady and principal—making sure he logged in for class on time—was a lot more work than I had expected. As the virus took hold, I took action and ordered a Peloton exercise bike. The monthly fee over a two-year window was reasonable, and again, worst-case scenario, if I was going to be locked up with my twelve-year-old son for a few months, I knew I would need to be able to work out. I had no idea how this situation was about to play out.

This was by far my best move yet.

Not only did the Peloton give me a great workout with fantastic music and upbeat instructors, but it also gave me the chance to give virtual high fives on the screen. No matter where everyone else was, we were able to cheer one another on and have a sense of normalcy. This was truly a godsend while we were stuck in our small apartment indefinitely.

Another week went by. More *no*s and then one *yes*!

The *yes* was from a smaller publisher, and the deal wasn't great. They cited the current pandemic as the reason for their offer. So, suddenly, I was convinced I had shopped my book proposal at the wrong time. If only I had gone to market six months earlier when the economy was stronger, I would have gotten more and better offers. At least that's what I thought.

After going down this track for another week, I started to open my mind to the idea that maybe this was actually the *right* time. Maybe, given the tremendous crisis we were all going through, this was *exactly* the right time for my book and the tools needed to overcome adversity and leapfrog villains.

That is what I chose to focus on. Done and done!

Immediately after that change of mind, I received two very strong offers from major publishers. This was an interesting conundrum to be in all of a sudden. How would I choose which publisher to go with? I remembered how I felt at my old job in corporate America when some people wanted me there and others didn't—it is a terrible feeling. I figured I would rather be with someone who is in it to win it with me versus someone who was only somewhat interested. I wanted *committed*, not just *interested*, and there is a big difference. And you should want that too.

I had individual phone calls with each of the publishers. They were each fantastic in their own right and both were all in. They both wanted me *and* the book. That was such a great feeling. I then took a step back and outlined the pros and cons of each. Then I called my agent and asked for her opinion, as she is the expert. In the end, we both agreed that HarperCollins Leadership was the right fit, and we agreed to the deal.

Then crickets.

It's so hard when you are new at something and you don't have anything to compare it to. I started to wonder if they didn't want me anymore. Can they do that? Will they pull the offer because of the pandemic? Was my timing terrible? Would I ever hear from them again? If you do this to yourself, then know that you are not alone. This old habit was rearing its ugly head in my life yet again. My entire life I have believed that no communication meant the worst-case scenario. I needed to remind myself that no communication is simply that—*nothing*. Instead of making assumptions and putting words into others' mouths, I needed to be patient, which is definitely my weakness.

I asked my agent what was happening. She reached out to them. Turns out publishing companies weren't set up to make the move to virtual, and they were far behind on getting contracts done. Mine was on their to-do list, but they didn't know when they would get to it. Patience was clearly something I had to work on.

The ups and downs during quarantine came fast and furious. Some days I was so grateful to have my son and our health and our great view. Cut to the next day when I would have a nervous breakdown and lose my mind because an expected package hadn't been delivered. My stress levels were at an all-time high, and I started to feel trapped in our small apartment. Our washer and dryer broke. The tires on my car went flat. My dishwasher broke. I forgot to make my son's lunch countless times when I had meetings and he was in his room on virtual Zoom school. The blinds in my bedroom fell off the rod and I couldn't fix them. *No one* would come to the house to fix them because of quarantine.

But that wasn't all. When school finally opened for in-person classes, they sent my son home with a fever and we were told to quarantine again. My son's dog died unexpectedly. My mentor passed away. The air-conditioning in my car went out. Two of the keys on my Mac keyboard broke while I was writing this book.

It felt like Murphy's Law, over and over again.

One day, my son and I got off the parking garage elevator to go to our car, and it was gone. I started bawling. My son stopped me and asked me why someone would steal our SUV when we were flanked by sports cars on either side. I stopped crying, then I grabbed his hand, and we walked right back to the elevator. We had gotten off on the wrong floor. These were not my finest parenting moments.

Then I remembered a strategy that I had taught myself in years prior:

When you're facing a difficult time, focus on something that you're looking forward to in the not-too-distant future. Once you reach that, create something new to focus on and look forward to.

Dylan and I focused on the upcoming Michael Jordan Netflix documentary *The Last Dance*, which we both were looking forward to. While I had started off quarantine mostly optimistic and healthy, that ship had officially sailed. I began eating worse than I had ever eaten before. I was downing entire bags of peanut M&M's, and before I knew it, I had gained at least fifteen pounds My clothes weren't fitting, but because we weren't leaving the house much, I was able to hide it.

That was a powerful realization for me. Going out in public was one way I held myself accountable. With that accountability removed, I realized I was going to have to create a new approach. With any goal, we need to hold ourselves accountable, and that clearly included me and my health.

With all of this insanity going on in the world around us, it also became evident that we wouldn't be going back to "normal" anytime soon, which meant I needed to find a new way to drive revenue from inside our apartment. I did a few virtual speeches and that was good. But they didn't pay anywhere near as much as my in-person events.

I needed more.

I decided to jump on my Peloton to figure it out. I am at my most creative when I work out—that's when my best ideas come to me. When are *you* most creative and likely to solve problems?

On the bike it hit me. I needed to go back to all of the messages people had sent me and see what the themes were. What things had most people ask me for and how could I package those offerings virtually?

Amidst great uncertainty,
we can always find certainty within.

I ran over to my computer and started combing through my LinkedIn messages. Within an hour, the answer was clear. Many people had been asking me if I consulted, offered executive coaching, or would be a mentor. That was it. I had no idea what someone would charge for these things, but I knew speed to market was critical to success. If you can solve a problem for others, then you have a product or service to sell.

I put a post on LinkedIn announcing my new group coaching program launching on May 1. In my post, I said, "You asked, and I have answered. If you are looking to be held accountable to achieve your goals, I got you on this one." I offered a 100 percent money-back guarantee because I knew I would work hard and overdeliver, and that would take the fear out of buying. Then I said, "Send me a DM if you want to sign up. I am only allowing ten people in this month, and the price is going up next month."

Within just a couple days, the program sold out!

I was shocked and excited, but there was just one thing: I had no idea what this new group coaching program would look like or how I would run it. Now what do I do? I went back to my old trusty friend, Google. I researched other, similar offerings and decided on a weekly group call each Friday, coupled with individual strategy sessions with me during the month. I knew I would need to collect an arsenal of testimonials from happy clients to promote and grow my new business.

We live in a review and recommendation world, and it is critical that you have testimonials of your work.Don't have any today? Start asking for them now.

That first month, I overdelivered for what I was charging. I was spending all of my time on one-on-one coaching calls, which was not a scalable business model. The good news is I received amazing testimonials to promote my business for the next month. I also learned the hard way that I had to pull back some of the offering to make the program work—both for me and for my clients.

That is the key. In any business transaction, both sides have to benefit. When one side benefits but not the other, it's not sustainable.

Now, how was I going to convey this change and not lose clients or revenue? Undervaluing ourselves is always the wrong answer.

I want to be perfectly clear: this time was beyond awful for everyone. My son would constantly remind me during the pandemic that everyone was suffering. I understand that we may have had it better than others, and that others may have had it better than us, but here is what I know: it was a very hard time for the world, and I am not minimizing that.

What I am trying to do is provide you with the understanding and beliefs you'll need to be prepared to take on the current and future uncertainties you're certain to encounter and build a better future for you and the ones you love. And no matter if you are a single parent like me or you found yourself alone and isolated or happily married or frustrated, we can all be proud that we made it through. Holding the belief that tough times are temporary and there will be better days ahead will carry us through the difficult moments.

KEY TAKEAWAY

Never rely on one revenue stream, one form of customer acquisition, or one means of delivering your product or service. Constantly challenge yourself to innovate how you monetize your business, acquire new customers, and solve problems for your client base. Change and uncertainty will be our constants, but we can always find our certainty within ourselves.

I would love to hear your story and answer your questions! To continue the conversation, join me wherever you are:

Twitter @_heathermonahan using #BAK
Instagram @heathermonahan using #confidencecreator
Linkedin @theheathermonahan using #overcomeyourvillains

CHAPTER 8

The House Heather Built

"A man is but the product of his thoughts.
What he thinks, he becomes."

—S. GANESAN

One day, when Florida was easing up on the virus restrictions, I decided to get a pedicure. I made an appointment for later that week. It had been a very long time since I had gotten one, and I was really excited about it. It's funny how something so simple can have such a positive effect on your state of mind. I knew that just getting out of my locked-down apartment for the afternoon would be liberating—a taste of my normal, pre-COVID life. Like everyone else, I was tired of being cooped up for so long.

The day of my appointment arrived, and I drove my car down a really beautiful road near where I live that has phenomenal homes, I mean—*absolutely* phenomenal homes. I did that because I wanted to see and feel the space and open area. If you're like me, living in a small apartment during quarantine, I'll bet you also set the same goal I did to figure out a way to get into a house with a yard before the next pandemic hits.

As I was driving down the road, looking at all these beautiful homes, I was thinking, "I want to buy one of these houses one day, when I can get my revenues where they need to be." As I was thinking about the beautiful home I wanted to buy, it reminded me of a story: the house that Heather built.

MY TIME IN
CORPORATE AMERICA

Years ago, when I was chief revenue officer at a publicly traded radio company, I had worked for the same CEO for fourteen years. He was the founder of the company. The company was fifty years old at the time, so obviously he'd been in business for a long time.

The CEO was having a housewarming party for the new mansion he had just bought on the Gulf of Mexico in Naples, Florida. The house was brilliant, exquisite, unbelievable. He invited all the executives from the company to attend, so there were a lot of us there. We were driven to the party on a private bus, and as we were getting off, everyone was saying, "Oh my gosh, this house is *amazing!*"

The house cost our CEO more than $30 million. It was huge, and right on the ocean. There was a guest house, a really cool tiki bar at the front of the house, a huge pool; the winding staircases were insane. To top it all off, Aerosmith performed for us. The whole thing was so crazy and so over the top.

So why am I telling you this story? Here's why.

After we all got off the bus, as we walked toward the mansion, a colleague from Atlanta said, "Oh my gosh, this is the house that Heather built."

I know my colleague meant well, but that really stung. I was chief revenue officer for the company, and my responsibility was to not only oversee revenue but to grow it year over year. I took on the challenge, and together with my team, we more than doubled revenue to over $200 million a year—despite the challenges of a declining market. During the fourteen years with this company, I had generated literally over a billion dollars for the CEO. I was proud of my accomplishments, but my colleague's point did not fall on deaf ears.

At that very moment, I realized where that $30-plus million came from for the mansion. It really was the house that Heather built.

Then I had an epiphany: "Well, if this is the house that Heather built, then why isn't Heather living here?"

I knew how to generate billions of dollars in revenue, and I knew how to do it successfully and repeatedly. But there was one thing different about him that I didn't have. Mind you, the CEO didn't work very much at this point in his career. He was basically coasting while I was out traveling almost every week, missing out so that I could generate the money to buy this mansion.

What was the thing the CEO had in him that I didn't? Why wasn't I the one living in this waterfront mansion?

The CEO had shared his story with me many times. He had grown up on a farm in North Carolina, then he spent four years in the army. After that he became a teacher and coach, and eventually a school principal where he earned $12,000 a year. The job was comfortable, but he thought he could do better. And he was right. One day, he decided to risk everything. He quit his job, bought a radio station, and started his own company, taking the risk of being an entrepreneur. He went out on a limb, having no idea what was going to happen.

I remembered a dinner party I attended with some good friends of the CEO a year or two before the housewarming in Naples. I knew the CEO's personal story—I loved the guy. He was a sweet man. One of his friends was sitting next to me at the dinner party, an older gentleman, and he said to me, "Heather, you need to know why George is so great." And I replied, "Well, tell me. I would love to learn why, and I want to hear from you."

And he shared the story with me.

In the 1990s, the internet boom had a big impact on the radio business, and everyone started selling their radio stations. "It was a scary time," he told me. "It was so uncertain, and banks were calling in notes, and everyone was saying that the radio industry was dead and over." Then he said, "So I sold my business, and it was the biggest mistake I ever made."

"So, what did George do differently?" I asked, genuinely curious about how our CEO had built such a successful business.

"He didn't sell off his radio stations. I remember telling George at the time that he was crazy because he wouldn't sell his stations. He decided to get funding instead. And so he pitched hundreds of bankers, doing everything he could to find the funding he needed to stay in business. Everyone told him he was crazy."

The man sitting next to me continued with his story. "George walked alone on the beach and contemplated, 'I'm risking everything. I hope I know what I'm doing. I hope that this works.' It was a huge risk, but as it turned out, he got his funding. He was one of the few people who stayed in the business, and George and his business just took off from there." Shortly after his decision, the internet bubble burst and George was able to acquire more stations and grow his company because of the risk he took.

So, while the comment "This is the house that Heather built" hit me hard, it also made me realize, "Yes, I know how to do this. I can generate the revenue. I can run a large company and succeed. But if I want to own the house, I need to roll the dice, bet on me, and take the big risk."

As I stood there in the mansion that I had built, looking out over the Gulf of Mexico, I realized what was different between the CEO and me. I hadn't taken the leap—to bet on myself, to take the risk, and to continue taking the risk when times were tough—the way that George had.

I went home from the housewarming party that night convinced that I would build my own house one day. For me and my family, not for someone else.

So there I was, driving down this beautiful road with all these mansions on the ocean in Miami on the way to my pedicure. I remembered the story of the house that Heather built, and I was motivated all over again. I committed myself to taking the leap.

I'm all in.

I make tons of mistakes all the time. I just sent out an email blast and there was an error in it. I heard back about it from lots of people. But my philosophy is that done will always be better than perfect, so it's not worth worrying about. I'm going to make mistakes, but just like George taking that walk on the beach, I know I'm not going to back off.

That doesn't mean I know how this whole thing is going to play out—clearly, I don't. Am I frustrated my company isn't further along and billing more revenues than it currently is? Heck, yes! But I also know I might be so close to that next solution, to that next revenue stream that's going to catapult my business—enabling me to start hiring full-time employees and really take off. I'm not at the tipping point yet, but I can promise you this: I am getting closer every day.

I envisioned George walking down the beach alone and making the crazy decision to stay in business. Everyone else was bailing out, and George decided to go all in. And it turned out to be the best business decision he ever made. I just keep reminding myself of that.

Yep, I am going to get that house.

Yep, I am going to build a company that generates millions in revenue.

I've seen the movie, I've done the work, and I'm going to do it again. But this time, for me. And this time not to make wealthy shareholders wealthier. This time to do more good in the world and help others while simultaneously building a successful business.

I hope that you go all in on *you* and take the chance, even when it's scary, because here's the thing: stepping into fear will always be the right answer. Believe it is possible and it will be.

KEY TAKEAWAY

Sometimes putting in the hard work is not the answer. When we pick our head up, we will see that the ones who succeed massively are those who took the biggest risks. What risk should you be taking?

I would love to hear your story and answer your questions! To continue the conversation, join me wherever you are:

Twitter @_heathermonahan using #BAK
Instagram @heathermonahan using #confidencecreator
Linkedin @theheathermonahan using #overcomeyourvillains

CHAPTER 9

Stick to the Facts— Memories Are Distorted

"Your beliefs become your thoughts,
Your thoughts become your words,
Your words become your actions,
Your actions become your habits,
Your habits become your values,
Your values become your destiny."

—GANDHI

Have you ever been part of a conversation in which your friends start reminiscing about a time in your life that you would rather forget? You try to smile and enjoy the conversation with everyone else, but in reality, you can't wait until your phone rings or you can excuse yourself without anyone noticing.

These times differ for everyone, but I bet you have one. Maybe it's your college friends remembering your first group trip, but all you remember is how you had gained weight and couldn't figure out what you wanted to do with your life. Or maybe it's your peers at work discussing when you all first started at your company, but what they didn't know was you always felt like you were about to be fired any minute that entire first year.

For me, one of the conversations I struggled with was reminiscing about high school.

So many people love that time in their lives. Some describe it as not having a care in the world. Others describe it as a period of self-discovery and growth. And others revel in being the star of the football team or the homecoming queen or class president.

That is *not* how I describe or remember it *at all*.

For me, junior high and high school were times when I felt less than others. I grew up poor. I had never felt smart—as I wrote about earlier, my sister was the "smart one." I had gained weight in my tween years and didn't feel good about how I looked. I struggled with independence. I didn't even like sleeping in my own room at night—most nights I would knock on my older sister's door and ask if I could sleep in her room.

My mother always wanted us to have great educations regardless of our financial situation, and she had applied for my sister and me to go to Worcester Academy, an expensive private junior high and high school. This was, of course, contingent on getting the financial aid we needed to pay for the school. My sister was a shoo-in because her grades were off the charts. I figured I would be left behind because I didn't have her level of academic achievement. In the end, we were both accepted, received financial aid, and were told we would be work-study students.

I had no idea what this meant other than I would be entering an entirely new world. I was stepping into a prestigious, private school world I had never been exposed to before. I was nervous about the whole thing.

At the start of the school year, it quickly became clear that the one thing I had going for me was that I was an athlete. I knew I felt confident on the field or on the court, so I leaned into that to get my footing. I didn't feel good around the other students when I wasn't playing. They all seemed so smart, so beautiful, and so rich. Yuck, my feelings of not being enough were intensified in this new environment. The school campus was beautiful, the size of many colleges. It felt overwhelming to me, and I felt so small.

Then things got worse.

I will never forget the first time they called the work-study students in for a meeting. Work-study students received financial aid but needed additional financial assistance. So the program allowed the students to work for the school to pay off the cost of tuition, books, food, and so on.

The work-study group was not very large since the school comprised mostly students from wealthy families. I know. You're thinking how lucky I was to have the opportunity, and I probably should have been thinking that same way. But I wasn't.

I wanted to hide. I already felt shame, felt less than the other kids. This work-study felt like someone putting a Magic Marker sign on my back that read "Kick Me"—like the one that high school kids tape to their classmates as a prank. Instead of Kick Me, however, the sign said, "Heather doesn't belong here. She can't afford it. So she will pick up the trash you throw on the ground in hopes she can afford to stay here."

It was a crappy feeling. So I did what I thought was necessary to survive it.

Any chance I could, I would dodge the work-study meetings or jobs I had that week. I would literally hide in shame. What this meant was that I would then put on a mask everywhere else I went. The more I would avoid my real situation and pretend it didn't exist, the more I would detach from the real me, which didn't feel good. In fact, it made me feel like more of a fraud. So I would have to work harder to appear like I fit in. I was trying so hard, but deep down I knew I was a fraud, and I knew everyone else knew it too. During this time, I was my own villain, but I didn't realize it until many years later.

I made it appear to work for four years. My grades were always average, never exceptional. Sometimes I would complete my work-study jobs, but mostly I would dodge them at all costs to keep up my façade. Those days were not good.

Finally, toward the end of my sophomore year, my sister was getting ready to graduate, and my parents told me I would not be returning in the fall for my junior year. I was devastated. This was all I knew as far as high school went, and even though I was a fraud, it was the environment I had now become accustomed to. My grades were average, and I didn't complete my work-study, so I was transferred to a big public school—Shepherd Hill High School—for my junior and senior years.

As it turned out, my grades were better at Shepherd Hill, and there was so much more financial diversity that I didn't feel afraid of people knowing my situation. But I had become so used to wearing a proverbial mask at my old school that I walked in my first day with that same mask on. I never loved Shepherd Hill, but I didn't feel intimidated by it the way I had by my private school. I missed my friends, but I learned to adjust, and life went on.

I kept in touch with many of my friends from Worcester Academy, and when I was launching my first book, a friend by the name of Jamie called. He let me know that he was now working at Worcester as a coach, and he wanted to ask me to address the entire student population about the importance of confidence.

Boom.

It was surreal. I was so grateful for the opportunity, but the idea of going back to this place that I hadn't been to since I was a kid was scary. It would force me to relive those awful moments of not feeling enough. Of not feeling good about who I was. Of dodging work-study in hopes people might not notice. That whole world was now behind me and I was about to enter into it again. Why?

Jamie worked out the details, and I flew to Boston, then made the hour drive to Worcester to stay with one of my closest girlfriends. Having Kelley there with me made it a bit more palatable, but I was far from excited.

The day we pulled onto campus my heart rate shot up immediately. A flood of emotions washed over me, and all I could remember is what a fraud I had been and how I had felt like I never belonged. But as we walked to the dean's office, something seemed different. The campus didn't seem as a big as I had remembered it. As a fourteen-year-old kid, that campus swallowed me up. Now, as a forty-four-year-old woman, it didn't seem as intimidating. Working in corporate America had put me in far more intimidating situations.

It's funny how your life experience can change how differently you view something. It is like seeing your first boyfriend twenty years later and thanking God that things didn't work out. (Ha!)

I was already feeling better. We walked over to the school assembly auditorium, and I was mic'd up to speak. The dean introduced me, and I took the floor.

This was the first time I had given a presentation to high school students. They were completely silent, which was odd to me. Usually, when I speak for a business, expo, or university, people are yelling or clapping—sometimes even snapping. So, right off the bat, I questioned myself. Was my message connecting with them? I shared how I used to feel when I was in their seats, and I told them my story about dodging work-study and feeling like I wasn't enough. Nothing. Crickets.

I hate crickets.

When I was done with the presentation, we opened it up for Q&A. There were only two questions. I figured I had bombed.

After we wrapped, we walked back to the dean's office. "What a phenomenal job you did, Heather," she told me.

"What?" I wondered which presentation *she* had attended. And then I explained to her why I didn't agree.

"High school students care so much about what their peers think," she explained, "that they never ask questions. It's great that they asked two." That I could relate to. When I went to school there, I was consumed with what others thought of me too.

That was a complete reframe. I wasn't aware of how differently a high school audience would respond compared to the older audiences I usually presented to. I felt better.

We walked over to the cafeteria I had eaten in every weekday for four years—from the time I was in seventh grade until my last year as a sophomore. It was hysterical! As I sat down to eat, I was bombarded by students who thanked me for speaking. The talk was a hit, and I felt so proud of myself for stepping into my discomfort, not knowing how it would go.

Ironically, the coach of my softball and basketball team was still there, and she saw me eating in the cafeteria. She came running over to me, yelling, "It's my MVP and my captain! Welcome back—I missed you so much!" I couldn't believe it! I had forgotten how well I had done there in sports. I had forgotten the impact this amazing coach had on me. I had forgotten all of the good because it had gotten lost under all of the fraud, lost under the mask I had put on and hid under. Lost beneath the distortion of the memories in my mind.

I had been carrying around all of the lies, and that was what I remembered. But buried underneath were all the facts I hadn't seen. I had been a leader on the field and on the court, and I had been a champion at that school that so intimidated me. But I hadn't celebrated or even acknowledged it because it had all been covered by my shame.

I promised myself that, from that moment on, I would *never* allow the shame and insecurity I felt growing up to affect my life as an adult. That was then, and this is now. The past is gone—it's dead and buried. There's only today. It's up to me to believe in myself and challenge those beliefs that no longer serve me.

KEY TAKEAWAY

The way we remember situations in the past is not the same way others remember them. Our inner beliefs and perspective at the time the memory occurs greatly influence how we re-create that memory in the future. Going back to a place years later forces you to confront the reality others remember versus the distortion you have carried with you. From there you can choose to let the distortion go. What memory are you distorting?

I would love to hear your story and answer your questions!
To continue the conversation, join me wherever you are:

Twitter @_heathermonahan using #BAK
Instagram @heathermonahan using #confidencecreator
Linkedin @theheathermonahan using #overcomeyourvillains

CHAPTER 10

Face Your Fear—It's the Answer You're Looking For

"It's not hard to create self-beliefs that produce a successful and happy life, the main job is to unlearn your limiting beliefs."

—MADDY MALHOTRA

Have you ever had that gnawing feeling of dread that comes with shame? Perhaps you cheated on a test and dreaded getting caught, or maybe you got a speeding ticket and didn't want anyone to know.

The bigger the shame and the longer you allow it to remain hidden, the more your dread intensifies—believe me, I know that's true. Hiding things from ourselves is a surefire way to crush our confidence. Just as shining a light on our shame allows it to disappear instantly.

In my desire to be a guest on as many big podcasts as I could, I landed a guest spot on nationally syndicated media personality Dr. Drew's show. Most people would be elated! But I am not most people. The idea of going live on a show where someone was a doctor, trained to identify patterns and responses as indicators of other problems, petrified me. I had been stuffing shame down deep inside me for a lifetime, and I had this gnawing feeling that once I was live on the show, Dr. Drew would see my shame and call me out.

I was a nervous wreck.

So I did what I had always done: I tried to distract myself. I made sure that week I was scheduled for back-to-back meetings so I wouldn't have a chance to think about it. While that worked for a while, in the end it was a flawed plan, because I found myself showing up for that big moment a bundle of nerves—sweaty palms, sweaty feet, and all.

Dr. Drew's team was nice, and the vibe was laid back, but I most definitely was not. I felt sheer panic that I was about to be exposed. I was afraid that what I had hidden from for a lifetime was about to be shared with the world. I didn't even know if I would have the courage to be honest—with Dr. Drew, or with myself.

After hiding for so long, it becomes difficult to imagine crawling out of that hole and owning your story. It seems overwhelming and unimaginable. I also want you to know that this is after years of counseling, inner work, journaling, meditation, hypnosis, anger, arguments, and nightmares. This was a lifetime coming.

You can either claim your shame
or your shame will claim you.

My shame had claimed me long enough, and I felt incredibly brave showing up for this interview. Dr. Drew came out in jeans and was kind and conversational, and at first glance, I didn't think he saw through me.

I felt relieved. Maybe I had him on a pedestal and maybe he wouldn't figure it out. I had fooled many people until this moment, including myself, and maybe I would be able to fly under the radar once again. But maybe, I thought, this was the time for me to stop trying to fly under the radar. Maybe this was the chance to finally set myself free.

I toggled the two paths back and forth in my mind. It had been exhausting always wondering if someone knew, or if I would be found out. My mind was racing, my hands were shaking, and we entered the recording booth. Dr. Drew asked me if there was anything off-limits that I didn't want to discuss.

"No," I replied, deciding in that instant which path I would take. Gulp.

Our conversation began and my voice was cracking. I was talking fast; clearly this was the most nervous I had been for an interview. Now, there is a fine line between feeling excited and feeling nervous, but this time I was definitely nervous—not excited. And there was no way to fool myself otherwise.

As our conversation went on, Dr. Drew asked me more about my family and my childhood. I could see in his eyes that he had seen what I had spent my life hiding from. But he didn't reveal it on the show. I am not sure if others listening to that interview picked up on it, but I definitely did. The interview wrapped, we stood up, and I asked for a picture. He agreed, but he then asked, "Can I ask you a personal question?"

"Sure," I replied, wondering if we were about to go farther down that path.

"Were you abused as a child?"

That was it. I knew he saw through me, and this would be the first time I verbalized my shame to someone I didn't know.

"Yes . . ."

Dr. Drew didn't judge me, didn't laugh, didn't make fun of me, or look at me any differently than he had when I first met him. Instead, he offered a suggestion.

"You know, if you could share this with the world, can you imagine how many people you will help?" He went on to explain the staggering statistics about child abuse—nearly one in every seven children are abused or neglected. Survivors of childhood abuse are more likely to experience mental health difficulties, including depression, anxiety, eating disorders, and substance abuse.

He explained to me that this was a massive problem and that I was not alone in dealing with this. He saw it nearly every day, and he saw just how damaging it was.

Dr. Drew asked me again if I thought I could share my story, knowing that it would certainly help others to come forward too. I told him I could, but I also needed to figure out how to do it without it impacting others in a negative way. I was scared. That was clear. I was afraid of being judged and afraid of what others would think of me. I felt embarrassed and like a fraud since I hadn't owned this sooner. I had a lot to think about, but I promised Dr. Drew I would share my story someday.

That was two years ago. For two years, I have thought about how I would share my story. How I would own my past and let go of my own self-judgment and fear of ridicule. I always ask myself what is the worst that can happen. But with this truth, my head came up with some crazy stories. So I decided to look at my *why*.

If I was going to do this, it would be for the other children out there who are suffering in silence. It would be to help even just one child, knowing that no matter what ridicule or judgment I would face as an adult, I could endure it. But what I could not endure was a child suffering alone thinking that there were no survivors out there.

I decided I could push through my fear and shame and own my past and the experiences I was so ashamed of. I would picture a child, a teen, or young adult who had suffered like me, and I would picture the person hearing my story and getting comfort from it. My *why* had become bigger than my fear. My *why* pushed me to write this chapter.

Just so you know, however, I wrote this chapter last, only after completing the rest of the book. Why? Because it was the hardest one for me to own up to. I believe in momentum, and for me that means starting with the easiest tasks and leaving the biggest, most difficult ones for last. This one was dead last.

I'll always remember hearing Oprah's story of abuse and how she overcame those awful experiences and became a voice for those who didn't have one. I also thought about the idea of *frequency*, how one person can share something and it can connect with you, while another person can share the same message—in different words or with a different example—and there is no connection. While my story may be similar to others, it carries its own frequency that has the potential to resonate with someone in a way they'll uniquely understand and connect with.

That is why it is so important that we all share our own stories.

So here is *my* story. I have mentioned that my childhood was not idyllic, but I will fill in some of the details now. My mom was a single parent until I was ten years old. She would have her parents watch me and my siblings when she was at work. At one point, we were living in a trailer in my grandparents' backyard, so it made sense.

My grandparents were not the doting and supportive kind of people you see in family movies. Their house was dirty and disorganized, and I had a creepy feeling every time I walked in. My grandmother was always angry and yelling at her dogs, which put me on edge because I didn't want to get yelled at too.

My grandfather was different. He always wanted to hug or kiss me or put me on his lap, and not in the way a grandparent should ever touch a child. The feeling I had during that time was like an out-of-body experience. I tried to detach from reality in some way when he would touch me or hold me down. There are no words to describe how scary it is to have someone who is supposed to protect you and care for you actually harm and sexually abuse you. I wouldn't wish it on my worst enemy.

I completely blocked out a lot of those early years of my life. It wasn't until I got divorced and jumped into serious counseling that I was able to start to deal with the trauma of this horrific experience. While traditional therapy helped, it was the work I did with hypnosis that finally let me relive these awful memories as an observer instead of a child victim. As I began to create distance between myself and the memories, I could begin to support myself and care for myself in a loving and kind way. Beginning to let others know what had happened to me as a child helped me to begin healing.

Sometimes we tell ourselves that so many people have already shared a particular message, so why does anyone need to hear from me? The reality is that someone out there *does* need to hear from you. Someone out there is on your frequency and will connect with your message.

They are waiting for you to share it and share it your way.

Besides making the decision to claim my shame, my decision to stop allowing my shame to claim me is the best, most empowering decision I have made yet. It's the difference between letting a single moment define you or seeing it as a defining moment in your life. It all starts with the belief that it is possible. Believe you can and you will.

KEY TAKEAWAY

As always, the answer is not only in confronting fear but moving through it. Sometimes firing our villain means letting go of our past and the things that have been burdening us. I realized I had been carrying my villain with me along the way. Then I decided to put that villain down, no longer needing to carry the past with me, so I could create a new future. The keys to success lie in confronting the holdbacks we have allowed for ourselves. Confronting those holdbacks head-on steers us toward where we are meant to go. What do you need to confront today?

Before we move on from the beliefs part, I need to share something very personal with you. My beliefs have been the biggest holdback in my life. I struggled with believing I was good enough, believing I was smart enough, believing I could build a successful career, believing in *myself*. For me, this has been the single biggest obstacle to my success—keeping me stuck in bad and sometimes toxic situations.

We all have the ability and opportunity to believe something different and to tell ourselves a different story—one that helps us achieve our goals instead of one that holds us back.

Choose to tell yourself a story about the beliefs that you know you want in your life.

Choose to end negative self-talk and start talking to yourself the way you would a child you love.

Choose to place reminders throughout your life for the moments when you are low.

Choose to focus on gratitude and use past successful moments as proof that you will have more of them.

Choose to believe.

I would love to hear your story and answer your questions! To continue the conversation, join me wherever you are:

Twitter @_heathermonahan using #BAK
Instagram @heathermonahan using #confidencecreator
Linkedin @theheathermonahan using #overcomeyourvillains

Turn Negativity into Neutral Thoughts

n an effort to give you as much value as I can in this book, I have decided to do something here that's a little different. I believe we can find a lot of value in the data that surrounds us. That data can be found in our social media, in assessing the messages we use, in reading over our journals, or through direct feedback from our audience or friends.

Over the last year, I have received a lot of feedback from my podcast, which I am so grateful for. When I get to hear what people like, I can try to give them more of it. Feedback is incredibly powerful.

When I first launched my show, my goal was to just get it live, knowing that over time I could evolve it and make it better. Along that journey, someone reached out to me and asked me to create a framework that would allow the listener to participate more directly in the work that the guest was sharing. This idea was brilliant, and I started creating exercises to accompany each show. Some of the exercises must not have been that meaningful, because I didn't get feedback on them. But some of them must have been very powerful, because I heard from a lot of people that they had had an impact.

This exercise is one of those impactful examples.

Trevor Moawad is a renowned mental conditioning expert who was named the "Sports World's Best Brain Trainer" by *Sports Illustrated*. I was lucky to get Trevor on my show, and his teachings on thinking in a neutral way resulted in some amazing feedback from my listeners. That's why I am including this exercise from his episode for you.

It has been a long-held belief that for people to be happy they should think positively. But let's be real: it's so hard to think positive thoughts when our emotions overwhelm us. The good news is there's a more practical way of thinking you can practice to relieve yourself from pressure-filled moments. *Neutral thinking* acknowledges that the past is irreversible and helps shift your mindset into something productive.

Neutral thinking drives your emotions into habits that enable you to achieve your goals. This activity will train your mind to think neutrally, which will allow you to make reasonable decisions and focus on what needs to be done to succeed in tasks. It will also show you the power of negative language and the difference between negative, positive, and neutral thinking.

ACTIVITY:
PRACTICE NEUTRAL THINKING

Positive thinking is a mental attitude in which you anticipate desirable outcomes. When engaging in negative thinking, on the other hand, you see the worst in everything. In the middle is neutral thinking, which allows you to accept that something has occurred, to move past it, and to think of what you can do next.

List the problems you are facing right now. Write positive, negative, and neutral thoughts about your issues in the corresponding boxes. Refer to the example below.

Problem: I have an exam tomorrow.
Negative thinking: I will fail tomorrow.
Positive thinking: I will pass this exam!
Neutral thinking: I will study all night to prepare for the exam.

Now you try:

PROBLEMS	NEGATIVE THINKING	POSITIVE THINKING	NEUTRAL THINKING

PROBLEMS	NEGATIVE THINKING	POSITIVE THINKING	NEUTRAL THINKING

What are the advantages of using neutral thinking in solving problems?

_____

_____

_____

_____

Have you ever experienced completing an overwhelming task by thinking that you're capable of doing it? How powerful have your thoughts been in that situation?

_____

_____

_____

_____

_____

WHAT YOU'LL LEARN
FROM THE EXERCISE

This exercise will show you the power of neutral thinking in transforming your thoughts and making your life better. Practicing neutral thinking enables you to move on from your past, make nonjudgmental decisions, and focus on what you can do to solve dilemmas. It enhances your creativity and encourages solution-based thinking, which are essential traits to have if you want to succeed.

Although thinking positive thoughts is good, it does not help you determine the things you have to do to succeed. It also presents you with broad statements that can be confusing when you have to decide what direction to take. Neutral thinking allows you to focus on what you can do to change your situation. It raises your performance, teaches you to let go of your emotions, and transforms your overall life.

The exercise also shows you the power of your thoughts. Your actions are based on your thoughts. If you think you can't do a task, you will not try to do it. You need to let go of beliefs that are holding you back. If you have to lie to yourself that you can do it, then lie. You won't know the range of your potential if you don't act.

PART II

ACTIONS

CHAPTER 11

A Thirty-Day Plan to Achieve Your Success

"Just remember, you can do anything you set your mind to,
but it takes action, perseverance, and facing your fears."

—GILLIAN ANDERSON

Have you ever felt overwhelmed looking at a big goal, unable to imagine what it would take to get there? If the road to victory looks too rough it might be time to try a different approach. One that simply focuses on the next thirty days and nothing further.

During all of the insanity and push and pull I was putting myself through, I could always escape by taking moments with my son. My son loves basketball, and I have spent many weekends in gyms watching him play.

One weekend I was watching Dylan play when he collided with another boy on the court. Yikes, that didn't sound good! I ran over to see if he was okay. He wasn't. Thankfully, I have an amazing friend in my life who happens to be a doctor. I called Dr. Green and asked him if there was any way he could get us set up with a doctor who could handle a badly hurt leg on a Sunday. Sundays aren't a great day to be seen by a doctor—the hospitals are extra busy, and staffing is often short—but my friend worked his magic and we were in.

Watching your child suffer makes everything else in the world seem so unimportant. All that mattered in that moment was him.

My parents happened to be in Miami for the weekend. I called them with the news, and they rushed over. I was so grateful to have them with me. They sat in the hospital with us—having support during tough times makes all the difference. We were told that Dylan had a broken leg. The doctor put him in a full leg cast and we headed home.

My son hobbled into his bedroom, and a few minutes later, I walked in to check on him. Of course, he was on YouTube, but I was blown away by what I saw him doing. "What are you up to?"

"Mom, I'm searching for my comeback song. I already found it— do you want to hear it?"

What? What was Dylan talking about? Here we are on the first day of the broken leg, and we have twenty-nine more days to go before we are back in to see the doctor, and Dylan is already focused on his comeback?

He explained to me that he had picked the song "Glorious." When he played it, he could see himself coming out on the court better than ever.

Yet again my child left me speechless. I was prepared to do my regular, thirty-day plan where we draw thirty boxes and check them off day by day, counting down to the final day where we get the cast off. But this little man had one-upped me. I loved it! Not only were we going to have our thirty-day countdown in which we record amazing things that show up each day, but we were also going to have a vision and a song that we would play so he could see himself walking out on to the court better than ever.

Creating this vision coupled with the music was incredibly powerful, and it put him in a positive mindset instead of focusing on the challenge of thirty days with a cast. And so, I ripped a page out of Dylan's playbook—when the first printing of my book sold out, I would play "Glorious" to celebrate!

Pick a song to couple with your vision. Play it before you achieve your goal to know exactly what it will feel like when you accomplish it. And then play it when you achieve your goal to celebrate. This works!

Some days, Dylan had setbacks, but every night when he got home, he would play his song and refocus on his comeback.

At one point, Dylan began to really struggle with his crutches—he couldn't seem to master them. His armpits were red and raw, and he was beyond frustrated. As I walked Dylan into the school one day, I explained the situation to another mom. She asked, "Why don't you get him a scooter for kids with a broken leg?"

What? They have *that*? How did I not know?

I am constantly reminded that there is *always* a solution to every challenge, every problem in our lives. It's up to us to find it.

Through a series of friends, we were able to borrow one. That scooter changed everything. My son was so happy! No longer did he have to deal with the crutches—he could get where he wanted to go much faster and more comfortably, which made the remaining weeks far easier for all of us.

Just because you haven't found the solution yet doesn't mean it doesn't exist—it just means you need to keep looking. Share with others what your challenge is and listen to their feedback and ideas. You might be surprised where you'll find the answer you're looking for.

While he recovered, my son was home a lot with me in the afternoons as he was on lockdown and had to stay off of his leg. One afternoon, he was scooting around the dining room and he saw a stack of books. One was Sheryl Sandberg's *Option B*. It was sitting on the coffee table along with a copy of my mocked-up first book.

When I first started writing, I didn't know what I would name my book or what it would be about, but I knew I wanted to write it, and I gave myself a deadline of six months to get it done. To keep me focused on my goal, I wrapped another book up with paper and signed my name on it. And when I came up with the title for that first book, I wrote it on the cover. I would look at my mock-up every day to keep my eyes on the prize.

Things become clearer the more real you make them. What you focus on is what you will create.

Dylan picked up *Option B* and held it out to me. "Mom, what is this?" he asked.

I responded, "It's just a book that I ordered that I want to read when I have time."

I got back to work. He laughed and said, "No, Mom. This is not a book for you. You don't need a plan B because your plan A is going to work. Let's get rid of this."

Seeing how my son believed in me more than I believed in myself was the encouragement and push I needed. I stood right up, took that book, and threw it in the trash. (Sorry, Sheryl.)

When I did that, not only did I build confidence in myself, but I also built confidence in Dylan. Yes, I could have stood there and explained to him that I was interested to learn from Sheryl Sandberg's heart-wrenching story and experiences, but that wasn't what mattered to me in that moment. I wanted Dylan to know that his belief in me meant the world to me. I also wanted him to know that his voice and opinion matter so much to me that I will act on his advice because he is worth it.

After living a decade of playing it small and being surrounded by people who wouldn't take action when I shared great ideas, I wanted my son to know that his ideas are great and speaking his truth is not only his right but his job. I want him to shine his light and own his truths, so in those moments when I catch him doing it, I'll jump right up to support and encourage him.

Spending so much time around people who didn't support and encourage *me* has taught me how important it is to support and encourage *others*. I am so grateful for that knowledge today.

A few months after my son's leg had healed, he had to write a paragraph in school about a time when he learned something new. This is what he wrote—I had it framed and I showcased it in our house so he can read it when he needs to remember what is possible:

When I broke my leg, I was afraid I could never come back as strong as I was in basketball. I couldn't walk properly when I got my cast off. It took me a while before I could walk again. I have returned to playing, and I am now playing better than I was before I broke my leg.

Sometimes things simply take time, and usually they turn out better than we have imagined.

KEY TAKEAWAY

Create a thirty-day grid to track your progress toward achieving your goals. Create the vision you have of yourself on day thirty and partner that vision with a song you will play when you come to realize your success. The key is to take action and to do it now.

I would love to hear your story and answer your questions!
To continue the conversation, join me wherever you are:

Twitter @_heathermonahan using #BAK
Instagram @heathermonahan using #confidencecreator
Linkedin @theheathermonahan using #overcomeyourvillains

CHAPTER 12

The Magic Is in Your Follow-Up

"Better remain silent, better not even think,
if you are not prepared to act."

—ANNIE BESANT

've had a lot of surreal experiences in the years since I was fired. I
didn't realize it at the time but getting fired may have been the best
thing for me. The old saying that when one door closes, another one
opens is really true. Stepping into your passion and your fear opens
up opportunities you may have never imagined before.

One of these opportunities was the chance to meet with the E!
team and discuss the potential of working on a show to empower
others. I had a friend who worked for NBC and happened to be in
a meeting where the E! people said that they were looking for new
talent that could talk the empowerment game. I was connected with
Anne, an executive at E!, and she wanted to talk with me about doing
the show.

My meeting with E! went well, but it just didn't go anywhere after
that. Anne loved my business background, but she needed to meet
with development to figure out where they could put me. Then
crickets.

I hate crickets.

A lot of times, when I'm introduced to a new opportunity, there will be a big wave of excitement and positive feedback, then nothing. Instead of feeling rejected, that's when I get to work.

I focused on achieving my goal of doing a show about empowering women, and I put it out to the universe that it was going to happen. One day, I was doing a segment on the local NBC station in Miami. While I was waiting in the greenroom, Heather—the station's sales manager—came in to meet me. She followed me on LinkedIn and had a career track in media that was very much like my own—she knew we would hit it off, and she was right. We had a great talk. The next day, I heard from her. She had been talking to the general manager about me, and they were interested in the idea of doing a show in which we would work with women to help them get ahead in business. I was so excited! We were moving into political season, so she said she needed some time because they were swamped; but they were interested. I was all of a sudden feeling *very* optimistic.

In the meantime, I was getting booked to speak on every stage I could possibly get on. Want me to speak at 9:00 p.m. on a Monday night at a college on the other side of the state? Yes! I will be there! Want me to speak to a group of start-up founders downtown at 7:30 a.m.? Sure, thanks for asking! I ran around like a chicken with her head cut off, but I felt grateful for every speaking opportunity I found.

This went on until, one day, my then-fiancé called me after a meeting he had just had. He shared with me that he had met with a former C-level executive from a major brand in corporate America who had left and was now a speaker and consultant working for himself. But here's the punchline: the former executive was making more money now than he ever did in corporate America.

"What are his revenue drivers and what are his fees?" I asked. He told me that this guy charged $40,000 for consulting, which included two phone meetings and limited email follow-up, and he charged $50,000 for a sixty-minute keynote.

I about fell over. My fees were a fraction of those. How was this former C-level exec able to command them? The answer was obvious: he had been with a major, well-known brand, and the company I worked for was smaller and not well known unless you were in the media industry. That must be the difference, right?

Brace yourself. That was not the difference at all.

My ex-fiancé said the difference was that I was undervaluing myself and getting paid whatever anyone offered instead of setting a fee and sticking with it. If I would value myself higher, then others would value me higher too.

Until we realize our value, no one else will either.

That was a tough one to hear, but he was right. As long as I took any speaking gig I could, no one would value my time. I apparently didn't value it, and I was sending that message out to the world loud and clear.

It's incredibly scary to be in a space where you are a rookie and you decide it's time to price yourself for the talent you have and the fees you want. It's a strange space where you need to get more experience, but you need to get paid too. Making the decision to set my fees at a level that reflected my expertise and the real value I offered was not easy, and I had to work into it.

At first, when people would lose their minds hearing my fees (and, believe me, they did!), I would walk them through different ways that they could reach the number. If the event had a large promotional budget, for instance, they could allocate some of that budget to promoting me specifically at the event, and I could give them credit against the fee. I got really creative because I knew I needed to start getting paid for the value I delivered.

Yes, I lost some speaking engagements as companies went for less-expensive speakers, but I did begin to see my value and I did begin to feel confident in my ask. Until you believe in and see your value, others won't either. The way I frame it for myself is that people are paying me for my twenty-five years of business experience I happen to be condensing into a sixty-minute keynote. This resonates much better with me than clients just paying me for a speech.

You are paid for your experience and expertise, and the ability to distill it into a shortened window for others.

Sure enough, I started earning more money for my speaking engagements, which was exciting. But I still wanted to nail down the show on my local NBC television station, as that would be another revenue stream for me. One of the things I have learned when you're working for yourself is that having multiple revenue streams is a must for staying afloat, as is constantly evolving and innovating your offerings for future growth.

I realized that I was starting to get a lot of interest online when I appeared on podcasts, so I decided that I should consider doing my own. That's when I reached out to my good friend Lauren, a friend and a client of mine back in my old radio–corporate America world. Lauren is one of the people who, when my phone number changed, immediately messaged me on social media to get my new number. She is one of the people whom I discovered was a real friend.

I asked Lauren if she would connect me with people in the podcasting world. She immediately thought of three different introductions she could make, and she shot out the emails. Lauren is the bomb! I had no idea just how much Lauren had helped me, but I would soon find out.

Lauren connected me with the head of PodcastOne, the largest podcasting company in the world. No pressure, right? As I considered my pitch, I envisioned the PodcastOne audience and how I could bring value to them. Sometimes we are rushed when we're in a job interview or pitching a client, and we simply highlight our attributes. That's a mistake. Showing how we can bring value to the other person and how we can help them achieve their goals is always a more successful conversation.

PodcastOne booked me right away for two shows as a test: *Lady-Gang* and *Dr. Drew*. I knew this was a big deal, but I didn't truly grasp at the time just how big a deal this was. I booked the dates and set up some meetings to maximize my trip to LA—one scheduled a few hours before my *LadyGang* appearance. As it turned out, that meeting ran late, and I realized it would be a miracle if I made it to *LadyGang* on time. I grabbed an Uber and prayed we wouldn't run into one of those infamous LA traffic jams.

In went the earbuds and I closed my eyes. I have a playlist that I use *every* time I am going into a stressful situation—my Fire Up playlist. Just like Pavlov's dog, I have conditioned myself to such an extent that when I hear the music I immediately see myself succeeding. Try it sometime—I think you'll be surprised at the results.

———

Create your personal playlist to get fired up when you are about to enter a big opportunity. Use it every time and watch how you begin to shift to "I am going to kill it!" mode.

———

Luckily, I made it to *LadyGang* in time. It was on the CBS lot, and I was shown to a tiny cubby of a room, dimly lit with a very low table where the women were sitting around and laughing. They were hysterical. I had just left a very opulent but cold and corporate environment, and here I was in a scrappy little room that was full of positive energy and laughs. I *loved* it, and I had no idea what I had stumbled into.

We had to start immediately because I showed up right on the dot. I was handed a water and headphones and Keltie introduced me.

These girls were younger than me, they were bubbly and funny, and they were excited to learn from me. Coming out of my last meeting, I couldn't have asked for anything better. The show was fun, and it felt like it went great! The things they struggled with, such as booking talent for their show and not knowing how to reach out to people, were easy for me. I shared with them how I ordered life-size cutouts of myself and shipped them to people in order to get a response when I didn't get one. They loved it and were going to do it themselves.

Thankfully, that ended my day in LA. Little did I know what was going to happen next.

Our show blew up! The show premiered its first week on the top-100 podcasts next to Oprah's podcast. Keltie had also shared with me off air that E! had come to her a year before offering the Lady Gang a digital opportunity to create content for them, which she had turned down. She told E!, "When you have a show for us that is our own show on E! TV, let me know. Until then we aren't interested." Sometimes you have to walk away from what someone offers you in order to get what it is that you really want. Well, guess what? E! came back a year later and gave them their own TV show. I was so happy for them!

Which brought *me* back to E! I decided to reach back out to Anne again and sent her the link to the show along with the photo of me and the *LadyGang* girls together. To my surprise, she responded immediately. As if she had never received the emails and voicemails I had peppered her with previously, she immediately wanted to reengage and told me she was so happy I had reached out. She listened to the show and loved it and wanted to set up a meeting for me and her head of development.

Finally! She made the intro, the head of development's assistant jumped in to set the meeting, and I sent my upcoming LA travel dates. The dates didn't work for them, and they asked me to let them know another time I would be back. I don't book LA trips unless something is serious—it's too expensive. This didn't feel secure, so I let them know I would keep them updated. The next trip I scheduled to LA, I sent the dates and they responded that those dates didn't work for them either. Then crickets.

Oh well—nothing ventured, nothing gained. The key is to keep moving forward and keep pursuing other options. This is part of my pipeline. It isn't dead—it's still alive, though on the back burner. I know that if I want to close one show, I need to be pitching myself for at least ten different ones.

Even though this hasn't come to fruition yet, here's what I learned from it and what you can take away from this experience: outcomes are not guaranteed; however, it is guaranteed that taking no action will deliver no result, no chance, and no potential opportunity. I will always choose to take action and start things in motion, never knowing what the outcome may be. At least there will be potential.

Remember: the magic is in your follow-up. And while this story is not just beginning, it is also far from over.

KEY TAKEAWAY

When a door closes, it is up to you to reopen it or leave it behind. Making a choice to revisit past opportunities and contacts is the tremendous difference-maker between achieving your goals or simply getting by. Don't wait around for opportunities to come knocking on your door—you might be waiting a long time if that's your strategy. Instead, follow up on them *now*.

I would love to hear your story and answer your questions!
To continue the conversation, join me wherever you are:

Twitter @_heathermonahan using #BAK
Instagram @heathermonahan using #confidencecreator
Linkedin @theheathermonahan using #overcomeyourvillains

CHAPTER 13

Eliminate Obstacles by Focusing on Solutions

"Things don't just happen, they are made to happen."

—JOHN F. KENNEDY

When I self-published my first book, *Confidence Creator*, one thing I figured out early on was that speaking engagements would help me sell copies. I also figured out that the bigger the speaking engagements, the better my chances of selling a lot of books. I therefore focused on finding a few big ones to target. One of those was the SHE Summit, which bills itself as "a global interactive experience to advance diversity, equity, inclusion, and social impact in the workplace and the world." The event attracts thousands of participants and is sponsored by Pfizer, Morgan Stanley, Aflac, and other corporate heavy hitters.

Here's the thing about getting into a new venture when you don't have the necessary contacts—you don't have the timeline, and you don't know how to get in. I had already learned from countless failed pitches to the wrong person; and I had learned that when I missed the deadline, small errors in trying to land speaking gigs meant a tremendous waste of time. One thing I didn't have was a lot of time, and the other thing I didn't have was a team of employees to help me increase my pitch counts.

The only thing I could do was ask my friends for help.

For years, I served on the board of City Year Miami, a charity dedicated to helping children and students in economically challenged areas succeed. I became great friends with the head of our Miami chapter, Saif Ishoof. He was funny, smart, and loved helping others just like I did. I definitely went above and beyond as a board member, and I loved doing it. When I first was fired, Saif is one of the people who immediately reached out to me, asking how he could help.

We had lunch and discussed my goals, and he mentioned that I needed to start speaking at as many different locations as possible so people could see me in action. Not only did he put an event together for me to speak at, he also invited me as a guest to attend a networking event that he thought might be good for me. Showing up is everything.

I had a tough time getting a sitter, and I really wasn't feeling like going to yet another networking event, but I knew I wanted Saif's help and I knew there was a chance I could meet new people who would open doors to new opportunities. Within fifteen minutes of my arrival, Saif introduced me to a few friends and told them about my book and my speaking. One of the women he introduced me to, Lori, happened to be best friends with the woman who puts on the SHE Summit.

Boom! Lori was sweet and friendly and genuinely excited to try to connect me. The next day, she sent an email to Claudia, the founder of the SHE Summit, and then crickets. I waited a few days and then reached back out to Lori, who let me know that Claudia was traveling for the summer. She also said she would get an email address of the woman who was running point on vetting speakers for the event. The next day, she sent me the email, and I immediately sent off a pitch.

Whenever I pitch myself for something, I know that I need to bring value, so I put myself in the decision-maker's shoes. If she is speaking to tons of prospective speakers, how do I stand out from the pack? I knew that my personal difference maker was my ability to be vulnerable and share my lowest moments. I also knew that if I could get her to read my book, it would be game over. I offered to send her, her team, and her sponsors copies of my book so they could consider it.

When pitching yourself for anything, put yourself in *their* shoes and be sure to add value.

She was so grateful and let me know they would be in touch in a month. I immediately wrote down in my calendar a reminder with notes telling me to reach back out one month from that day and reference the conversation. A month passed and nothing. I followed up and still nothing.

Then, one day, I received a letter from Bacardi International, one of the sponsors of the SHE Summit. The woman who wrote the letter, Kim, said that she had read my book and that it changed her life as she was making some very big life moves and addressing some major struggles. She wanted me to know how grateful she was that I had sent her the book.

I immediately googled her name and found her email address. I sent Kim an email explaining how happy I was that she loved the book. I told her I was excited to meet her, and I asked for her help. I asked if she would consider reaching out to the SHE team, telling them what she thought of the book, and requesting that I be a keynote speaker for the summit.

She did exactly that.

A few days later, I got a call notifying me that I would be one of the keynote speakers at the SHE Summit. Soon after I called Kim at Bacardi to thank her for her help, I got an email from the SHE Summit explaining that they were having problems getting copies of my book through their book partner, Books and Books. They needed me to figure out a solution.

When you self-publish a book, there is so much freedom, which is great. But there are tons of issues when it comes to dealing with companies that usually only deal with traditional publishing houses. Apparently, SHE Summit had partnered with Books and Books, and they were managing the on-site selling of all books. They couldn't get copies of my book as it was self-published. SHE Summit connected me directly with their client at Books and Books—let's call him Tony—and I asked if I could come in to meet him for an in-person meeting. I did that because it's easy to tell someone no when you're on the phone, but it's a lot harder to say no face-to-face. Saying no via email is basically a forgone conclusion.

Tony wouldn't meet with me in person, but we did have a call. He explained they didn't accept self-published books for a couple of reasons. First, I had self-published my book with Amazon, their main competitor. Second, the only way they could order my book was through a portal that they typically didn't use because the prices weren't discounted enough for bookstores.

Ugh. I knew I needed to get Tony to *want* to help me, so I shifted away from what he didn't like about my situation to explain to him why this was so important. I told him about getting fired, about starting my first company, about all of the mistakes I had made, and about how it was so key for me to speak at the SHE Summit and have my books there for sale. I desperately wanted my books on the table for attendees to see.

Then Tony focused in on the one issue that was causing him the greatest problem. "The problem really boils down to this," he told me. "Financially, your book doesn't fit in here because the one portal that I can purchase through doesn't offer a large enough discount to allow our company to make any money."

> Once we are clear what the problem is,
> we can find a solution.

Problem solved. Once I was crystal clear on his problem, I figured out a solution.

"Tony, if your real problem is simply you need a greater discount, tell me how much more you need."

> "Tell me" is a sneaky command that will
> get you the information you need.

"It will have to be four dollars less per book for me to do it."

I shared with him that I had cases of my book sitting in my house, and when he ordered through the portal, I would bring him enough books at no charge to bring his total cost in line with what he was asking for.

He was quiet for a moment. Then he said, "We have never done anything like this before."

"How about this?" I offered. "I will sign every single book that you have of mine and every book that I bring in to make the math work. Now, that has to add some more value, right?"

Tony laughed and agreed to work things out as we discussed. Another challenge, another solution found. On to the next one.

The day of the SHE Summit, a car picked me up to take me to the event. Just then, I received an email from the law firm I was booked to speak at the following week. "Heather, we did as suggested and ordered books for our event from Books and Books, and my assistant just returned saying they didn't have any in the store."

I was livid. I was sending people to Books and Books and they didn't have my books in the store. How the heck was that the case? Should I have followed up? Yes! I should have gone down there myself to confirm. But it's just me, and there is far too much work to do in a day. I have had to let some things go. Did this mean that I was heading to the SHE Summit with thousands of women in attendance and no *Confidence Creator* available to purchase? I called Tony immediately and got his voicemail. I asked him to call me back. Then I sent an email asking why there weren't any books in the store.

I could feel my face getting red. I was going to an event to sell my book and now my book wasn't available.

This was unreal. My mood went from being upbeat and excited to upset and angry. I knew I couldn't walk into a speech upset and angry, so I was going to have to shift my perspective and fast!

The quickest way I can shift in a situation like this is to put on my speaking playlist; it's the same playlist I use to fire me up when I am going to speak for any event. The minute I begin to hear the music, it puts me into my excited zone, and I begin to replay in my mind the other successful speeches I have made, how well they went, and how happy I was. I decided to block out this issue for the time being as there was nothing else I could do until Tony responded. My music was blasting, and I was calming down.

Walking into the event, I could see the tables with books for sale all over the place. I braced myself for the bad news that Books and Books had dropped the ball. As I walked to the greenroom to get mic'd up, I glanced at one of the tables at the front of the room, and there was my book—an entire table full of books, in fact. *Confidence Creator* might have not made it into the store yet, but it sure had made it to the summit!

As I walked onto the stage and scanned the room, I could immediately feel that the crowd's energy was low. I knew I needed to take action to change it. I saw a DJ on the side of the stage, but no music was playing. I walked up to the DJ, told him I was going on, and that I needed him to blast my theme song as I walked out, right up until I started speaking. He laughed and asked what song. "Started from the Bottom" by Drake, of course!

Boom! He hit the beat and the place went wild. Just as my playlist does for me, the music changed the energy in the room in an instant.

I started jumping up and down and clapping and ran out onstage—laughing with my hands up. I shouted into the mic, "Are you all going crazy for me or is that for *Drake*?!" I was off and running!

When you can engage your audience quickly, you can keep them with you for the duration. I gave my keynote, and right before the end of my speech I said, "For all of you who want to know more, my book *Confidence Creator* is for sale up at the front of the room, and I will stay after and sign everyone's books. Thank you for your support!" I had been told by so many experts that selling from the stage is cheesy and a no-no, but when I looked at everyone's face, I could tell they wanted to talk and would want a signed copy.

That day, my book was one of the only ones to sell out. The woman from Books and Books said it was because I let people know it was there and that I would sign it. Sometimes you need to go against the grain and follow your intuition, because you will probably be right. When you focus on solutions, you'll be able to overcome even the most difficult challenges. Never give up!

And by the way, Books and Books came through and have been a fantastic partner to work with.

KEY TAKEAWAY

It is just as easy to focus on potential solutions as it is to focus on the current obstacles. By continuing to focus on different possibilities, we can find ways to move around the obstacles and still achieve our goals. What solution can you create today? Now, make it happen!

Hold yourself accountable right now and let me know what action steps you are taking:

Twitter @_heathermonahan using #BAK
Instagram @heathermonahan using #confidencecreator
Linkedin @theheathermonahan using #overcomeyourvillains

CHAPTER 14

Do the Things That Create Confidence and Avoid the Things That Chip Away at It

"You'll never plough a field by turning it over in your mind."

—IRISH PROVERB

One day, during a business trip, I jumped in an Uber and checked my messages. One of the messages was from a woman I knew from social media, Michelle, and she wanted to know if I would consider speaking at an event she was holding close to my home in Miami in another couple of weeks. The event looked small, but I have learned that, when I show up for things, opportunities can happen. So I really try to make the effort to show up whenever I can.

Author note: In the event that this left you scratching your head as I have been preaching about raising your fees and valuing yourself and your time, I need to remind you that this book was not written in chronological order. The book is in three parts—beliefs, actions, knowledge—and there are moments like this one where the story you are reading now actually happened before I had raised my fees and started saying *no* to unpaid events. Here's the thing: sometimes you've got to do what you have to do until you can do what you want to do. There is no doubt that I wanted to get paid for all of my events when I first started, but the reality was I needed footage of me speaking, needed testimonials of my work, and I wanted to refine and test my message. So, when I started out, I worked for free even though it wasn't the end goal. Speaking for free is what got me started and allowed me to see my potential. Making the transition wasn't seamless or easy and there were moments where those lines were blurred. As my business grew and I had a roster of paying clients, I began to see it as unfair for me to speak for free for others when I had great clients that saw my value and paid me for it. I began to realize if I wanted to be taken seriously, I would create an option for unpaid events: I created a pre-recorded video that I would send to anyone that had an unpaid event in lieu of me speaking. This protected my paying clients and provided value for those in need. Now, back to the story . . .

I have also learned that if I can help out another person, and I am not already committed to doing something else, then that simple act always pays dividends even if you don't see it at first.

I fired back a *yes* and explained I would waive my speaking fee for her. But I would need her to create social media support for me so I could receive some value for my services. This is another thing I have learned since going out on my own. Not everyone in your social circle may be able to afford the kind of fees that corporations can afford, but that doesn't mean that your value isn't there. It is key to get paid for your services and respect your value. One way I have found to help friends out and still get my value is by creating an agreement where I am paid in social media services, management, or support services. The exchange of value is key in growing any business.

When I began doing speaking engagements for a fee, I knew I was a rookie, and I definitely felt like one. I accepted many speaking engagements for which I hadn't even asked for a fee because I didn't know what to charge or how to value my services. At some point, I realized that I couldn't continue in this way—I needed to actually start making money doing the speaking or I needed to drop it and find another income stream. I felt confident I would deliver a compelling presentation that would provide value to my audiences, and that meant I needed to be compensated.

I was starting to feel stronger and more confident in this new role as a speaker. What I didn't know then was that I was fishing in the wrong pond. One of the main reasons I wasn't getting paid for my speeches was because I was speaking for people who didn't pay speakers to speak. Time to change ponds.

A couple weeks later, I was getting ready to give my speech at Michelle's event. I was keeping my expectations low and was focused on doing a favor for a friend. I drove out to a warehouse-style gym forty minutes from my house and walked in. There was a large group of women getting ready to do a workout. Michelle had told me to wear workout clothes, but she had not told me much else. When I walked in, Michelle gave me a big smile, introduced me in the nicest way, and gave me the floor.

By this time in my speaking career, I had spoken so many times that I felt extremely comfortable jumping into situations in which I didn't know anyone and then sharing my story. I could now anticipate where the audience would laugh and where they would gasp. I always try to tailor my talk for the specific group, and this day I focused on the moms in attendance and on sharing stories I knew they could relate to in order to help them create their confidence. There is no substitute for experience. Practice and experience in small venues is what gave me the confidence to walk into bigger ones, so I was happy to be there.

After my talk, we began a workout—actually, a boot camp, and it was a beast. All of the ladies, including me, were struggling. I loved it! I had never thought I was going to get a fantastic workout in addition to giving a speech, but that was what was happening. We were all high fiving and having a great time.

At the end of the workout, Michelle thanked everyone for being there and asked that everyone give me a shout-out on social media. Most of the ladies stayed after we had wrapped, and we all introduced ourselves. I met so many fantastic women. One, Jasmin, asked me if I knew Grant Cardone. A few years earlier, I had done a show for Grant—arranged through a mutual friend—when he needed a media expert as a guest. I also knew that he was hosting the largest sales expo in Miami—so large that it was three days long and was being held at Marlins Park with an audience of thirty thousand people. Jasmin told me that she was hosting a show on Grant's platform, and she wanted to know if I would come on the show as a guest.

Well, this was serendipitous! I was dying to land a spot on Grant's stage for his 10X event at Marlins Park, and I knew the more I could put myself in his circle, the better chance I would have of making it happen. "Jasmin, I would love to!"

Another woman, Jenn, overheard Jasmin and me speaking and jumped in and asked, "You must know Grant's wife, Elena, too, right?" Well, yes, I did know her from the taping we had done, and I would love to find a way to see her again. Jenn smiled when she told me that she was going to a gala with Elena that weekend and had an extra ticket. "Would you like to join me?"

"Of course I would!" I didn't hesitate an instant.

These are the moments I remember why I show up to help out friends and why I show up, period. This was a huge opportunity for me to reconnect and do it over and over. Frequency is key in selling anything, and in this instance, I was selling myself. Now I would be seeing Elena socially and then a week later I would be at Cardone Enterprises. 10X stage, here I come!

I secured a babysitter for the Saturday event, then looked through all of the dresses in my closet to figure out what I would wear. It had been a while since I had been to a gala, and I didn't know if what I had would fit or how anything would look. This is when being a woman is challenging. We don't always feel great about our bodies, or we wonder if clothes from years ago will still fit. The struggle is real! Thankfully, I found a dress that I hadn't worn in two years and it still fit! Problem solved, and I was ready to see Elena again.

Heading out to the event, I was trying to temper my expectations. Imagine, I am going to a gala with a woman whom I had just met a few days prior, joining a group of women I did not know, and trying to find a way to spend some one-on-one time with Elena Cardone, whom I hadn't seen in years. Yikes, this may not go well! I decided to look at this like a work situation and set some goals.

What was my ultimate goal? To reconnect with Elena and have a conversation with her about getting on the 10X stage. To do that, I would need to find a way to get any assistance I could from women I didn't know. People can be funny sometimes. You meet someone and you click instantly, and other times it is more work. I was committed to making this work, so I was planning to go in with a big smile, ask lots of questions, and be as friendly as possible to make others feel comfortable and connected with me. People like people who are interested in them.

Luckily Jenn and I really hit it off, and she kindly introduced me to a large group of women. A few of the women looked as though they were in the same situation I was, not knowing anyone else at the event. I made a beeline for them and let them know they weren't alone—we were in this one together, and we were going to make it fun.

When Elena arrived, she made a point to walk up to each of the attendees to thank them for being there, supporting her event, and filling her tables. When Elena got to me, I reminded her that I had done her husband's show and that she and I had spent the day together three years earlier. She remembered me and asked if I wanted to go with her to have our picture taken. At just that moment, one of the gala organizers told me I needed to register first. Shoot! I hadn't signed in and registered and couldn't enter the event until I had. Like cattle, a group of us all scurried over to the end of a line and waited to enter the event. By then, Elena was nowhere in sight. I had my eyes wide open and was waiting for my shot, and the next time I was going to make my ask.

A little later, I saw Elena again, and it looked like she was getting ready to leave. I jumped up and asked if I could speak to her for one minute. She was exceptionally gracious and kind and agreed. I explained to her that since I had last seen her so much had happened.

A few months before the gala, I was fired, and I had started my own company and become a professional speaker. She was so encouraging and complimentary.

Then I made my ask. I explained to Elena that I had recently spoken for the WNBA and BNY Mellon and had been the keynote speaker for the SHE Summit. I told her I really wanted the chance to take the 10X stage. I shared with her that I felt it was important to have more women on the stage, particularly women who had experience in corporate America and as entrepreneurs. I let her know that I would bring so much value to her audience by way of sharing my lowest moments and how I overcame them and how the audience could do the same.

Then I stopped talking and waited. She smiled. She was genuinely happy for me. Then she shared with me that she and Grant were very clear on things at work and at home, and she was not the ultimate decision maker at work. She also explained that Grant had a right-hand man named Jarrod who was running point on the conference and that he could make the decision to add me. She agreed to connect me with him and get my reel over to him and help in any way she could. She also mentioned that she had a speaking engagement the following weekend and would love to see me there and have my support. I agreed and was excited she invited me. We exchanged info and then she was gone.

Goal accomplished, I went back to my table. We finished dinner then all went our separate ways. The long process of attempting to get on the 10X roster had begun, but none of it would have happened if I hadn't agreed to help out my friend Michelle by speaking at her small event. Helping others always pays dividends, even if we don't see it immediately. Keep doing the next right thing, and then when your opportunity arises, jump on it!

KEY TAKEAWAY

In the past, I would wait for others to open the door to opportunity for me. I now know that *I* am the key to open any door. I have the power to unlock any opportunity and so do you. You have *always* had the power inside you. If last year was the *right* time to do it, now is the *only* time.

I would love to hear your story and answer your questions!
To continue the conversation, join me wherever you are:

Twitter @_heathermonahan using #BAK
Instagram @heathermonahan using #confidencecreator
Linkedin @theheathermonahan using #overcomeyourvillains

CHAPTER 15

Create Opportunity
by Taking Action

"Thinking will not overcome fear but action will."

—W. CLEMENT STONE

Whenever you are going to the next level, there are going to be setbacks, fears, opportunities, self-limiting beliefs, and all of the old ways of thinking we have become accustomed to. It's easy for me to write these words right now. But every time I am in the throes of this, I completely lose perspective and panic.

It was late afternoon, and I was writing when I got a DM on my LinkedIn page. As I read the message, my jaw dropped. It was from a Harvard professor asking me if I would consider being a guest teacher for his class. Yes, Harvard was calling. What!? I was certain I was getting punked. One of my friends must have created a ghost account and was just tormenting me. Or maybe it was Ashton Kutcher?

In this moment of disbelief and self-doubt, I googled the name of the professor. Turns out, John Westman was listed as a professor on the Harvard website. I next went to his LinkedIn page to verify his ties to Harvard. Check. So I responded to him that I was happy to set up a call and discuss his offer.

When John called, I was beyond excited and nervous. I still couldn't understand why I was getting tapped to teach at Harvard when I could never have gotten in there as a student. Can you say imposter? I had immediately gone back to my negative self-talk, remembering that I was the "social one" who belonged only in the "sales lane." All of those old self-limiting beliefs kept rearing their ugly heads when I was attempting to go to the next level.

It takes incredible self-awareness and discipline to stop yourself in these situations and realize that this way of thinking is part of your past. That you are facing your fear means you are growing, and that is an amazing thing.

During our call, John told me about all the fabulous guest teachers he had had in the past, and he walked me through the course syllabus and plan. He was incredibly detailed, just the way I thought a professor at Harvard would be. Detailed, direct, smart, exacting.

That is when I had to ask, "John, I am beyond blown away that you have asked me to teach your class at Harvard. However, I have two questions that I need answered. One, how did you find me? Two, why me?" I was suffering from major imposter syndrome.

John told me that someone he knew shared with him a video I had posted on LinkedIn, and he thought I would be a good addition to his class. The post he saw was of me sharing some sales tips and a story about something I had experienced that day. I have learned over time that sharing personal experiences and stories engages others and often encourages them to share the post. Once John viewed my post, he followed me back to my profile page, where he saw my accomplishments and track record in business.

What I learned in that moment was that taking action and creating something starts a chain of events that you may not even see happening but that can eventually affect you in a very positive way. I took a chance creating a video and sharing it on social media, and because of that, I was going to get the opportunity to teach at Harvard. What can you do today to start a chain of events to elevate yourself?

I remind everyone of this: LinkedIn is the place to showcase your highlight reel. It's not the place to hold back or be bashful, because everyone else is shining their light and you want to put your best foot forward too. Put some effort into having an updated headshot and optimize the words in your profile description. List any awards you have won and accomplishments you have achieved. Most important, list the recommendations and reviews you have received. The world in which we live today is a word-of-mouth society in which people will see your content, your website, and your claims, but they will defer to what *others'* experiences have been with your product or services.

John was impressed with my successful career in corporate America and my pivot into the entrepreneurial world. Can you imagine that? The girl who had been fired just over a year earlier was now being seen as valuable enough to teach at Harvard. These moments are odd for me, and I naturally go back to the low moments in my life. It's hard not to let them take over. However, I am aware of my natural reaction and know that there is a good chance things will work out. I have to keep reminding myself of that—it doesn't come naturally. Being a rookie can be hard. Self-doubt is everywhere.

Hearing that a professor at Harvard was impressed with my experience was eye opening. Equally as eye opening was when John shared that me being a woman who made it to the C-suite—and transitioned successfully to becoming an entrepreneur—was unique and would add a lot to his class. Hearing how he saw me and how I could add value to his course bolstered my confidence. Seeing how others see us through their lens always makes us feel better. Posting about this experience opened my eyes to even more.

Immediately after we had met and worked out the details, I posted how excited I was to teach at Harvard. I shared that I felt nervous and doubted why they would want me. Seeing the responses to that post made me realize something. The typical response I got was, "With all of your success in business and experience overcoming adversity, why wouldn't Harvard want you? Textbook experiences are limiting. Real-world experiences are so much more powerful."

Honestly, I was still in shock. I just kept thinking that I could have never gotten into Harvard for college, but now this Harvard professor wanted me to teach a class there. I felt like a total imposter. In that moment, I realized I had "Harvard" on a pedestal. It was time for me to take the school off the pedestal and put everyone on an equal footing.

My next call with John came after he sent me more course materials to review. This call was much easier. Making that deliberate decision to take Harvard off the pedestal helped me ease my fears and become more grounded. Besides, the second time doing anything is always easier.

We had a good call, and at the end John asked me a favor. "Heather," he requested, "please do be sure to share some low moments or fails you had in your career as my students are already intimidated by your success."

What?! These Harvard students were intimidated by *me*? I couldn't believe what I was hearing! I had been feeling nervous that I didn't deserve to be there, and they were feeling nervous that I was coming and was "so successful" in their eyes. When you listen openly to others, take everyone off their pedestals, and leave your past stories in the past, you'll be surprised to find that there's a reason why they asked you to be there. You were asked to attend the meeting because you add value, and you are wanted. You are in the room because you are part of the group and they want you to be there. We can all add value and learn and contribute something.

The Harvard class went great! But rather than tell you just how wonderful it was, I'll include the words of appreciation I received from John:

Thank you, Heather for your insightful, thoughtful, authentic presentation today for our class. Your success stories, practical advice, and positive energy are inspirational!

Send up the Bat-Signal. Let's go! Of course, I asked for a testimonial!

The only way you can ever be an imposter is to deliberately show up as someone other than yourself. If you bring the real you to the table, you'll *never* be an imposter.

KEY TAKEAWAY

Taking action and creating content starts a domino effect that will pay dividends for you. When you shine your light and put yourself out there, others will be drawn to you. Share your expertise in your own quirky way, and you may be surprised at who reaches out to you. The key is to always be doing things that move you forward, not backward.

I would love to hear your story and answer your questions!
To continue the conversation, join me wherever you are:

Twitter @_heathermonahan using #BAK
Instagram @heathermonahan using #confidencecreator
Linkedin @theheathermonahan using #overcomeyourvillains

CHAPTER 16

Own Your Vision, State Your Claim

"Take action to see reward.
Do nothing and be ignored."

—MATTHEW E. FRYER

t's funny how opportunities start to show up when you get yourself out of your funk and focus on the good things in your life. In addition to journaling, one of the ways I watch my progress is through the photo roll on my iPhone or through my Instagram feed. Taking some time to look through these photos shows me just how far I have come. I liken it to living with a child. You see your child every day, so you don't really notice how she's getting taller and more mature. But when you bump into an old friend and they see your child for the first time in a year, they're blown away by how much she has grown.

When we are so close to ourselves and our lives and our day-to-day routines, we often don't give ourselves the recognition that we should. Using the stories on your 'gram to showcase your year will keep your accomplishments front and center for you. When you get your mindset right, big things will begin to happen.

I was in a *fantastic* mindset a couple years ago when, early one January morning, I woke up to an email from Steve Harvey's producer asking me if there was any way that I could be on the show the following Friday. I know this much: when a big opportunity comes knocking, you don't just say yes, you say *hell, yes!* No questions asked, no checking flights, no looking for a sitter. Just say yes and figure out the details later.

That email didn't just come out of the blue, however. The year before, I had the opportunity to meet Steve and pitch myself in person for the show. In that meeting, I shared everything about me that I thought would resonate with Steve's audience and exactly how I could bring them value. I explained that I had been fired by another woman and how heartbroken and devastated I was—I didn't know how I was going to move forward. I shared my fear around whether I could write a book and get it published. I said that I was certain my story would inspire others to make the change they may have been considering but thought it would be too hard.

The producer loved my pitch, and he told me I could be on the show as a onetime guest, or maybe even a recurring guest on their weekly Straight Talk panel. It was my choice.

I thought about the two options and quickly realized that a recurring spot would be much more valuable than a onetime appearance. So, I said, "Panel!"

"Oh—okay," the producer told me. "Go home and watch some of the panels—we'll be in touch when we have an opening."

Ugh. I had just blown it. I should have taken the onetime guaranteed appearance and then hope that they would want to book me for the panel later. I tried not to beat myself up over what had happened. Listen, in any situation when you are given a choice, you need to go with your gut, knowing it is a risk. Nothing ventured, nothing gained, right?

I flew back home to Miami, worried I would never get that face-to-face opportunity again. That was the first week of October. I reached out a few days later, sending another signed book to the producer and his assistant, and I emailed a follow-up thank-you note.

Crickets.

I then emailed the assistant whom I went out of my way to get to know. I always do this. By making people feel important and learning about them, they will look out for you. She replied immediately. "He got your email," she said. "He will get back with you when he has something."

I've been in the media biz for years, and I know the kiss of death when I hear it. And that was what I just heard!

Waiting is not my thing, so I decided to lean into my *LadyGang* recommendation and fire up a life-sized cutout of me. I emailed the producer's assistant a note explaining to her that it was coming and that I would so appreciate her putting it in the producer's office.

This time I didn't hear back from *either* of them. In my mind, this opportunity was dead.

Then came the January email from the producer, and everything changed in a flash. After I replied with an immediate *yes*, I consumed every possible panel show I could find so I would know what I was walking into.

Anytime you do something new—especially if it's new and *big*—then you're bound to be intimidated. You're bound to be nervous. Anxious. Worried. Maybe even a little scared. I don't care who you are, this is just a fact.

I was intimidated, but I knew that I was going to be on the show no matter what. As I watched the shows, I began to envision myself on the couch there with the rest of the panel. The more I could envision myself there, the more real it became. And the more real it became, the more possible it seemed to me that my appearance would go really well. I was excited, and that is an understatement!

I am a creature of habit, so I like to be in places I am familiar with, and I like to be around people who support me. Whenever I visit Los Angeles, I always stay at the same hotel. That's because of someone who works behind the front desk. The first time I stayed there, my room had a broken A/C unit, and it was awful. I phoned the front desk to complain and Marcus answered. Marcus was polished and professional, and he attempted to calm me down. I was irate, however, because I had an early morning meeting and I was petrified I would not get any sleep. I demanded the A/C be fixed immediately or that I be moved to another room.

Marcus sent an engineer right away.

Long story short, once the engineer arrived, it was obvious to me there was a bigger problem. The engineer looked worried. He told me it would take twelve hours for the unit to thaw out, and the A/C wouldn't be operational until then. I immediately called Marcus and let him know that I needed to be moved into a room with a working A/C. He apologized and told me he had no other rooms to move me into. I explained my situation to him—that I had just flown in from Miami and had a huge meeting first thing in the morning. I needed his help. I also told him I knew a lot about the hotel business, and I was certain he could work his magic and figure something out for me.

I told Marcus I had confidence in him.

Fifteen minutes later, he assigned me to a new room. From that moment on, Marcus had a never-ending, loyal client. After I found someone who would look out for me, I refused to stay anywhere else. Finding people who treat you remarkably well means you need to treat them remarkably well too.

So when I booked a room for my Steve Harvey appearance, I told Marcus all about it. It turned out that he happened to know Steve and some of the people on the panel. He shared all of his insights with me and told me he would see me at the hotel—and that he was root-ing for me! That feeling of knowing I was not alone and that I was supported—almost three thousand miles from home—was priceless.

After a good night's sleep at my favorite LA hotel, I took a shower and had some breakfast. But about two hours before I was supposed to head over to the studio, I started to feel really nervous about my appearance. Now, if you have ever struggled with anxiety, you know this is the worst. Luckily, I've struggled with anxiety in the past, so I knew how to treat it: by *tapping*.

This is the process of tapping your fingers on the meridians located under the surface of your skin while stating your fear, acknowledging the fear and upset, and affirming that you still love and accept your-self. My tapping points are the same each time. I start with the top of my head, then move to above an eyebrow, then outside of the eye, under the eye, under the nose, under the lip, collarbone, under the arm, and then finally I tap both of the bottoms of my palms together. It's that simple.

For the next ten minutes, I tapped. And throughout the process I repeated out loud, "Even though I feel anxious and nervous about going on the show, I love and accept myself. Even though I am afraid of this unknown, I love and accept myself."

After five minutes, all my anxiety was gone. I was ready for anything!

My good friend Nikki couldn't make the trip to LA with me, so I asked Diane who did my makeup if she would please come to the show with me. When going into stressful situations, it always makes sense to ride with a good wingman. The car the show sent over picked us up at the hotel right on time. That was the good part. The bad part was it smelled like an ashtray, the water bottles in the back of the car were half gone, and the traffic was horrific.

It *was* LA, after all.

To get my mind in the right place, I put my earbuds in and lis-tened to my playlist that always gets me into the right mindset. I use it every time I go into a new or stressful situation. It makes me remember all of the other times I felt afraid and made it through to the other side okay and in one piece. I pulled out my lavender hand-wipes (that scent calms me down) and I started to visualize sitting on the couch with everything going great and me happy. I stayed in this state of bliss the entire ride. Smelling my lavender handwipes, rocking out to Kendrick Lamar, and visualizing myself being happy on Steve Harvey's couch.

That did the trick!

We walked into the studio and were led to the green room. While the show producer (a woman, not the same producer who invited me onto the panel) briefed me on what to expect, she laughed and told me that my views were entirely different from the other women's. Then she gave me some really good advice: "Don't let them talk you down or talk over you. They are strong women—stand up for yourself!"

I let her know she had the right girl. She had no idea how long I had been pushed down at my old job and what I did to stand up for myself. "Don't worry," I told the producer. "I've got this."

Let's go!

I went backstage, Diane in tow. I was grateful to have her with me as the other two women on the panel had each brought their own entourages along with them. Both had been on the show before, they knew each other, and their teams knew each other.

Yikes, I was odd woman out!

When I start feeling like that, I ask myself, "What can I find to compliment someone on right now that will build some common ground between us?"

Kandi Burruss from the *Real Housewives of Atlanta* was one of the other panelists, and she was wearing the most amazing, most electric blue skirt I had ever seen. I loved the color! I tapped her on the shoulder and complimented her on it.

"Really?" she said. "I was hoping it wasn't too extra. Good, thank you!"

Connection made; I instantly felt a little better. That's when Steve walked into the green room and hugged both of the women. He then walked over to me and introduced himself. He was nice and professional, and he told me to relax and just be myself. That was one thing I knew I could do!

We walked out into the studio and planted ourselves on the couch. It was a bit confusing at first, but I quickly found my voice. And once I did, I felt good—*really* good. I showed up as me and spoke my truths and the audience responded. Things weren't perfect, but I was happy with the outcome. I *owned* it.

The show wrapped and we were led back down to the greenroom where Diane was waiting for me. She gave me positive feedback and I felt better. We were walking to the car when the producer's assistant ran out to me. "You did a great job, Heather!" she said. "We would love to have you back!"

Wow. That meant *everything* to me. No one has any idea the stress or fear that confronts you when you are trying to get to the next level in your career, your business, your life. Finding ways to create confidence in those moments is what will save you every time, because self-doubt and fear have a way of creeping back in. Be alert to when fear and anxiety rear their ugly heads and make a point of finding your happy place.

When you own the outcome, you'll take it to the next level every time. By the way, I never got back on that show. *Steve* was canceled right after that and the door closed. No matter what people see on the outside, there will always be a lot more letdowns on the inside that the world may not be aware of. When one door closes, we have to get back up and open a few more.

KEY TAKEAWAY

Having big dreams and huge goals can be scary. Writing those goals and dreams down as claims that will be happening will get you thinking about these things in a new way. Holding yourself accountable to achieve your dreams is key to your success. Whether you recruit a close friend to check in with you or put it out to the world on social media, you need to find a way to hold yourself accountable and not look back. If you don't jump, your wings will never have a chance to appear. It is your time to jump!

I would love to hear your story and answer your questions!
To continue the conversation, join me wherever you are:

Twitter @_heathermonahan using #BAK
Instagram @heathermonahan using #confidencecreator
Linkedin @theheathermonahan using #overcomeyourvillains

CHAPTER 17

Don't Hide from the Haters

"The greatest prison that people live in is the fear
of what other people think."

—DAVID ICKE

A re you ready for a rude awakening?

Some people like to pretend that being a perfectionist means that they are held to a higher standard—it makes them somehow better than you and me.

I call BS on that.

Perfectionists are just like you or me.

They're scared.

Scared they will be judged.

Scared of making a mistake.

Scared their work or ideas won't be accepted or praised.

———

When you strip perfectionism down,
you are left with fear.

———

Here's a question to ask yourself: Would you rather have published an imperfect book—with just three errors—or would you rather be lying on your deathbed someday, telling your son or daughter that you had the *perfect* book in your mind but were never able to write it?

Done will always be better than perfect.

Yes, my first book, *Confidence Creator*, has three mistakes and I am so proud of them!

Would I rather have *no* book and *no* mistakes? Hell no!

See fear as a green light that means go!

And that rings true for the video you want to create, the email you are hesitant to write, or the question you want to ask in your next meeting. Done will always be better than perfect, and doing it will build momentum for you!

The more I have thought about fear and perfectionism, and the more I have stepped into my fear, the more I realize that so much of this fear is rooted in fear of haters—the villains in your life—and their judgment. When you begin to shine your light, the haters will come for you. They love nothing more than trying to bring you down. It reminds me of turning on a light when you're outside and the bugs start swarming around, stinging, biting, and leaving behind big, painful welts.

I think of this every time I do something different and the haters come for me. I imagine the light and the bugs swarming, and it makes me smile. Yes, gross analogy, but you get the point. The haters don't come for you if you don't turn on your light. If you decide to play your life small, without your light shining, no one will come for you. But then, guess what? You'll be left in the dark.

We were not put on this earth to hide in the dark. In fact, we are here to make the world a brighter place, and that means shining the light we were given.

One of the first big experiences I had with this was when my first book came out. I knew the haters would be coming for me because I did something different and unique. I was prepared to celebrate the haters—until one hit me pretty hard.

Now, pump the brakes before you detach here and say, "This is *exactly* why I won't write a book or do something that calls attention to myself!" Here's the sad truth: I also had haters when I got my first promotion at work, when I got fired, when my son ran for class president and won, and when he lost. My point is you don't have to write a book to deal with haters. Haters will be there no matter what you do. No matter if you are succeeding or failing. They are coming.

When you launch a book, people can review your work on many sites. Knowing that we live in a review-and-rating world, I knew it would be important to gather great reviews for my book. But I didn't think about how much a negative one would hurt. Here is some perspective: When you have hundreds of decent reviews, one negative review gets lost in the pile. No biggie. But when you launch, and have only a few, one bad one can be game-changing. That's what happened to me. And that can happen to anyone when asking for reviews of your work.

When I launched *Confidence Creator*, I steered everyone I knew to Amazon to leave a rating and review. What I didn't know as a first-time author was that the book-review site Goodreads is also very important. It had a couple of good reviews of my book already, and then someone created a ghost account and left a one-star review. I wouldn't have even known about it if a friend hadn't seen it for herself and reached out to me.

She sent me a text and a screenshot of what the faceless ghost account had left:

1*

That crushed my overall rating on Goodreads, taking it from a 4.5 to a 2.5 rating.

I was livid. I knew my book wasn't perfect. But I also knew that my book was good, and it absolutely did not warrant a one-star review. That the review was submitted under a ghost account that had just been created strongly suggested that this was an attack by a hater—sadly, probably someone I knew.

Get ready for the irony; here it comes.

Remember the woman—my villain—who thought she had fired me from my executive job when I actually had fired *her*? Her birth name is Barbara, and guess what? The name on the ghost account was Barbara. No photo, no history of reviewing anything else, no information at all. Just a one-star review for *Confidence Creator*.

Once I put those pieces together, my anger started rising. I thought, if this lady was actually my villain hiding behind a ghost account, I needed to call her out on it. So that's exactly what I did. I decided to go to social media and post this:

When you decide to shine your light and be your authentic self, know that haters will come. Taking the risk to CREATE and INNOVATE will anger those that haven't or leave them jealous or uncomfortable, and NONE of that has anything to do with you.

On GOODREADS someone has posted a 1* review of my book. It's a new ghost account named "Barbara" no information, no history, no picture and no reviews other than to review *Confidence Creator* with a 1* rating.

A fan messaged "Barbara" on the review, *what was it that you didn't like about this book?* SHOCKINGLY, no reply.

When I shine my light, I've been confronted with haters and ironically *Confidence Creator* is about OWNING your voice and being CONFIDENT in who you are.

So, for "Barbara" I hope you read *Confidence Creator* today and begin to create confidence for yourself so you can own your 1* or anything else for that matter because it's yours and you should be confident in your opinions, even when they aren't with the crowd.

Own who you are and shine your light and you can and will when you create your own confidence.

Hoping this post inspires "Barbara" to read the book, so she can own her profile and her voice, which I will applaud, 1* and all ☺

Rock your #confidencecreator

That single post did things I never could have imagined.

It inspired people to go to Goodreads and flood my book with positive ratings and feedback. Until this incident occurred, my strategy had been to ignore haters; and frankly, that is usually the best approach. But I discovered that it *can* pay off to selectively leverage negative reviews and comments left by haters and villains.

Calling out this hater ended up helping me.

Another time a hater came out of the woodwork to attack me happened when I posted a photo of me on social with these words:

———

I don't lose.
I either win or learn.

———

When I wrote the post, I had no idea that these words came from Nelson Mandela. I had even googled the quote before posting it to see if it was attributable to anyone specific. I had seen it all over the internet with no author, and I hadn't seen it attributed to Nelson Mandela. So I posted the image with the quote without attribution.

Soon after, a woman commented on my post: "That is a Nelson Mandela quote."

Okay—that was news to me, but I was grateful that the woman had let me know so I could correct the error. I thanked her, and in the text portion of the post I added, "The quote in the image below is attributed to Nelson Mandela."

Case closed. Or so I thought.

The woman then commented back, "What you did in the post is not good enough—you must delete this post now."

I thought that was crazy. And why would someone whom I don't know—who doesn't work for the social media platform—dictate to me how I attribute someone's quote and what is acceptable to them or not?

I didn't delete it, and the post started going viral because the community saw the thread and started jumping in with their own opinions.

In the end, I left the post where it was, but I also created a new post with Nelson Mandela attributed in the image *and* in the text portion of the post. I also told the story about what had happened: I hadn't known who the quote was attributed to, and when I found out, I made the proper attribution. I went on to explain that someone didn't think that was good enough, so I was now reposting it—with the proper attribution *both* times.

That new post went viral and here's why: everyone deals with haters and naysayers and people telling you what you did wasn't good enough—so people could relate. In the end, if you move through with good intentions and make mistakes and own them, 99 percent of people will relate to you and understand.

Here's the funniest part of this story: turns out the quote isn't actually attributed to Nelson Mandela. During the final editing process, it was brought to my attention by one of our editors that this quote has been attributed to numerous people and isn't sourced properly. Knowledge is power and it would have been powerful to know this during the exchange; however, I am still pleased with how it all played out. Takeaway—be careful before you attack others. You never know, you may have bad information.

Last year, I had the chance to go on Gary Vaynerchuk's podcast, and one of the topics we dove into was haters and how Gary approaches them. Here's what he told me: "Judge the judgers."

That really had an impact on me. Instead of being judged and then judging ourselves, why don't we look to the person pointing the finger and wonder why they are doing it? What's their real motivation? The reality is, they are probably struggling, angry, or jealous of something. When we can try to find empathy and understanding for those people, we can make the world a better place.

I have never been attacked by those who are incredibly happy in their life, and I try to remember that. Sometimes I put the haters to work for me, sometimes I ignore them, and sometimes I feel badly for them. But one thing is for certain, I never let them stop me.

It will always be harder to create and innovate than it is to critique and judge. I will take the harder, more rewarding road every time, and I hope you will join me: building a solid foundation with the bricks that are thrown at us.

KEY TAKEAWAY

Haters are a sign that you are succeeding. Haters are a sign that you are shining your light. Haters are a sign that you are not vanilla. Let's celebrate when the haters come! You can also take action by leveraging haters' comments to elicit help and support for yourself.

Would love to hear how you handle haters!
Share with me wherever you are:

Twitter @_heathermonahan using #BAK
Instagram @heathermonahan using #confidencecreator
Linkedin @theheathermonahan using #overcomeyourvillains

CHAPTER 18

Defeat the Villain Within

"Do you want to know who you are? Don't ask.
Act! Action will delineate and define you."

—WITOLD GOMBROWICZ

While it may be easy to spot the villains in our lives we need to leapfrog—the toxic boss, the boyfriend who's always trying to drag us down, the guy doing his road rage thing in the shopping center parking lot—it's never as easy to notice when *we* are the villain in the moment. It is not easy because we have blind spots—things we just can't see unless we're looking especially hard for them. We have blind spots with our weaknesses, our routines, the things we do subconsciously, and much more.

It's only through self-awareness that we can begin to take on the worst villain there is: the one living between our own ears.

Back when I was in corporate America, I taught myself to dim my light, not even noticing I was doing it. For example, if I did my hair and wore an amazing red dress, some of my coworkers would become angry. I knew that was the case, so I would dial down my look to ensure I didn't upset others. Yet there were also days when I was so frustrated that I would dial up my look—a silent protest to make it known I wasn't happy with the muzzle that had been put on me.

When you work with toxic people who are trying to hold you back, you begin questioning everything about yourself. This is why it is so important to *fire your villains*! I spent so much time creating a watered-down version of myself in hopes it would help others feel better that I truly became a lesser version of who I really was. I had buried the real me deep down inside.

Here's the simple truth: if you are in a room with people who are trying to hold you back, *you are in the wrong room*! This is your alert message: there is a room somewhere else where you can show up as the real you, bright light and all, and the people there await your arrival so they can cheer you on. This is a truth! The key is leaving the wrong room right now (don't put it off another second!) and finding the right one.

I used to walk into a room hoping the people in it would like me. Now I walk in hoping I will like them. (*Jedi mind trick.*)

A funny thing happened to me a few years ago that made me aware that *I* might be the one who was holding me back.

I had been on the board of the City Year Miami charity for nearly a decade while I was in corporate America. Helping underprivileged children has always been something very near and dear to my heart. I could see my younger self in them—the girl who was standing in the checkout line at the grocery store and who had to put half the food back because she didn't have enough money to pay for it. I wanted to be there to guide the kids and help them see their real potential.

After a while, City Year Miami asked me to speak at some of their events. This was something I loved to do, and I was happy to grab the mic every time they asked. One event they asked me to speak at and emcee was the annual Women's Luncheon. I was incredibly honored to be asked, and I invited some of my closest friends and colleagues to attend. But that's where it stopped. I didn't share the event outside that small circle of friends and colleagues—I definitely didn't plan to post about it on my social media.

Why not? Because, while I saw many men post about their awards or their big speaking gigs, I just knew that if I did, people would

attack me. I was convinced the haters would make a point of showing up and calling me out. All my excitement and gratitude would be
taken as proof of my lack of humility. I wasn't willing to risk it.

When the day of the event arrived, I was more nervous than normal. Instead of my standard talk or intro, I had decided to give a more
personal talk. I had decided to share that as a child I struggled with
poverty, low self-confidence, and a lack of guidance. Like anything,
the first time you do something new is the scariest, just because you
haven't done it before. There is a fine line between fear and excitement, and I needed to keep telling myself: I feel excited for this talk!

The next time you feel fear, make the
decision to say out loud how *excited* you
are instead. Watch the shift happen.
There is a fine line between fear
and excitement.

I somehow made it through the speech, and I waited for the
crowd's revulsion I was certain would come after my deeply personal
revelations. Here was this high-powered corporate executive reveal-
ing that she grew up poor and had lived in a trailer.

The crowd loved it.

Today I have spoken about so many low moments and shared so
many things I used to feel shame about that I don't even think twice
about it. But it took practice—it was hardest the first time, and each
time it has gotten easier. Today, I look forward to it. That is because
of what happened next.

While I was making my presentation and barely keeping it
together, I didn't notice what was happening in the back of the ball-
room. In the far corner, my then-assistant, Kim, had leaped up and
started livestreaming my speech on Facebook. She hadn't told me

she was going to do it, probably because she knew I would have never agreed to it. Maybe she knew it was the little push that I needed to put myself out there to the next level. Regardless, I am so grateful that she did.

I finished the talk, and as I walked back to my table, so many amazing women told me how moved they were. Some told me of their own challenging moments in life and how my speech connected with them and reminded them that they are not alone. I knew right then that the risk I had taken was the right one.

Stepping into your fear is always
the right answer.

We began packing up and heading out to get into our cars. That's when I glanced at my phone and noticed that I was getting more notifications on my Facebook app than I had ever seen. "What's wrong with Facebook?" I wondered.

I opened the app, and to my surprise I realized what Kim had done. Not only that, but hundreds of people were responding to it. Before I could read their comments, I wanted to hide under a table and find a way to delete what she had done. I immediately thought the worst. Hide under a table? Was I four years old or forty-three? I knew deleting the livestream wasn't going to make it go away—I needed to face the music and look at the post.

I jumped into my car with one of my colleagues, Carolyn, who needed a ride to the airport on my way home. I told her what was going on with my Facebook app, and she was cracking up. Carolyn had been a supporter of mine for a long time, and while I was in panic mode about the livestream post, she was absolutely comfortable with it. She was able to see that my fears were not real and that everything was going to work out much better than I expected.

I handed her the phone as I was driving and cringed as I asked her to read the responses to me.

"So proud of you!!"

"Go Heather!"

"You are an amazing speaker!"

"I can't believe you didn't tell me about this. I would have been there to support you!"

"Why didn't you invite me? I would have loved to be there live!"

"Heather, seeing you do this tells me I can do this too. Thank you!"

"You are shining, girl—keep shining!"

"Thank you for sharing your struggles. It makes us all feel like we are not alone."

There were so many amazing comments, but one in particular made me reframe my whole attitude that posting about your wins is a negative thing. The next comment came from a single mom who had been holding herself back. She said that seeing me up there onstage showed her that she, too, can go for more. She thanked me and told me to keep an eye on her because I would be seeing something big from her soon.

That's when I finally understood it. It's my duty to post and share about my wins, just as it is my duty to share about my fails. When I reframe it in that way, I give others the chance to see the potential within them.

It's not about me. This is so much bigger than me.

If your post about an achievement can inspire just one person, then it's worth it. Make it about that one person and not about you.

Fast-forward to 2020 when I launched my executive coaching business. I had the opportunity to work with equal numbers of men and women on this exact same topic. One woman explained it to me like this: "Sharing that I have won an award just feels icky to me."

I challenged her to remember times in her career when she shared something great with someone and they were happy for her and inspired by her. She did as I suggested and did remember such times. Although she wasn't 100 percent convinced she should share her wins, she decided to make the leap, and she received amazing feedback from a lot of people. She had helped many of these people realize that they, too, had the potential to do more. She was so happy for this outcome that she now doesn't hesitate to share her wins, and she does it with pride.

A couple of months later, I met with one of my male clients who had just written a bestselling book. *Entrepreneur* magazine had just named it one of the seven must-read books for 2020. I was so happy for him! It was such a major accomplishment, and it reflected his fantastic work to elevate others. I let him know that we needed to showcase the book *everywhere*—as a feature on his LinkedIn profile, posts on his blog, podcast interviews—anyplace we could get it noticed.

I was not expecting my client's reaction.

He put his head down and told me he didn't feel very comfortable with this strategy because he was a very humble man. That made me lose it. I explained to him that this has absolutely *zero* to do with humility and everything to do with elevating others. I reminded him of his amazing work to help others and that he needed to share this so they would know what was possible for them. He finally agreed. As a result, it's having a positive impact on many, many people. I am so proud of him and his work.

This reframe also applies to making an apology. Instead of apologizing for everything, which makes it all about *you*, reframe your apology to make it all about the other person. Thank them for their patience. Tell them how grateful you are for their understanding. Reframe "sorry" into gratitude.

KEY TAKEAWAY

If you are feeling nervous or uncomfortable shining your light, make it about the one person whom you can inspire or help, and stop making it about you.

Before we move on from the Action part, I need to make you aware of some of the things I know about people who don't take action.

1. Perfectionism is a holdback and it is also just a cover for *fear*. Remember: fear is a green light that means *go*!

2. If you are waiting for permission to go for it and take action, consider this as your permission. Permission granted!

3. Many people will come up with stories about why they *can't* take action. I am challenging you to tell yourself a different story now. A story that shares how you *can* take action.

4. Many of us suffer from imposter syndrome. Here's the reality: We are all beginners the day we start doing something new. We aren't imposters, we are all simply beginners in this moment in time. Everyone started as a beginner the very first time, including you, so get started. A year from now, when you look back on today, will you regret taking action or will you regret not taking action? (I think I know what your answer is going to be.) Get moving.

I would love to hear your story and answer your questions! To continue the conversation, join me wherever you are:

Twitter @_heathermonahan using #BAK
Instagram @heathermonahan using #confidencecreator
Linkedin @theheathermonahan using #overcomeyourvillains

Regain Confidence and Assert Your Value

You know, I am digging deep to bring you as much value as possible, and that means including some top exercises from my podcast. Cal Fussman is a world-renowned American journalist, author, speaker, and podcast host. But, more important to me, he has become a friend. While Cal is incredibly talented in the world of interviewing—having personally interviewed former presidents, notable athletes, and celebrities—he is not experienced in the art of selling or promoting himself. In many ways, that has come across as him not valuing himself the way he should.

That was the topic that he and I got into when I had the opportunity to have him on my podcast. This is also a great example for all of us that, while you may be an expert in one area, you can simultaneously be a novice in another.

Products are priced by factoring in the costs of raw materials and production and then adding a profit. Use the same approach when you price your services. You have to treat your service as a tangible product worth paying for. But how do you do that in uncertain times? The key to asserting the value of your work is through your confidence in your message and your story. Believe in your ability to contribute to others' lives and businesses. If *you* don't believe in your value wholeheartedly, why would anyone else?

One of the challenges I had along the way as I began to work as a speaker was understanding and justifying to myself how I could charge so much money for a sixty-minute speech. I knew one thing for sure: if I didn't believe I was worth it, no one else would be willing to pay me for it.

Now that makes much more sense to me.

Conversely, if you are young and have a unique perspective on an older, more traditional business, you can see your value proposition as the unique lens that you see things through applied to the traditional business model. That lens allows you to see what others before you have not been able to realize. That lens allows you to connect the dots that seemingly were not obvious to those who came before you. That lens is what allows you to innovate what has never been before.

Discover how you can create opportunities, especially when you find yourself outside of your comfort zone. Learn how you can pivot and adjust by solving problems for others and charging for your valued services. It's also essential to connect with your audience or clients through your stories. To get more information on the power of questions and storytelling, you can listen to the conversation with Cal Fussman on the *Creating Confidence* podcast, complete this exercise, and take a step closer to regaining your confidence.

ACTIVITY: CREATE YOUR OPPORTUNITIES

UPGRADE

Why is it important to ask questions and ask for help?

_____

_____

_____

_____

THE PITCH

Do you have a business opportunity in mind or an idea of what you want to do? In the space provided, list these business opportunities and ideas.

_____

_____

_____

_____

_____

KNOW YOUR MARKET

List the opportunities you think you have, or you think you can create. In the next column, identify your target market for these opportunities.

MY OPPORTUNITIES	MY MARKET

PRICE POINTS

Complete the table below. In the first column, indicate how much you think your service is worth. In the next column, you can ask other people how much they are willing to pay you for the same service.

HOW I WOULD PRICE MY SERVICES	HOW MUCH OTHER PEOPLE WOULD PAY FOR MY SERVICES

WHAT YOU'LL LEARN FROM THE EXERCISE

Upgrade is an activity that reminds you to seek opportunities. Some things in life will not be handed to you quickly. Sometimes you need to ask for these opportunities, and there is no shame in doing so. Your curiosity and persistence in looking for answers will reward you with knowledge and opportunity, which are both an advantage for you.

The Pitch is the beginning of your journey. This activity gives you an overview of where opportunities might be waiting. There is no big or small idea—the important thing is never to discourage yourself from trying and learning new things.

Know Your Market is an activity that will streamline your business activity. Once you know your opportunities, which could either be selling products or offering your services, you always have to consider who your audience or customers are. Think of those who would be interested in your offer. Know and understand their story so you can approach them with familiarity, and your transactions will be more comfortable and successful.

Price Points is an activity that will help you estimate how much you can charge for your services. If you are having a hard time putting value to your work, this activity might help you create a price point or a range for a particular service. Identifying your prices can be challenging, especially if you know that people are struggling. Nonetheless, don't ever undervalue your work. People who need your help will always see the value you can provide in solving their problem for them. What problem do you solve?

PART III

KNOWLEDGE

CHAPTER 19

Carry Your Expertise
to New Arenas

"To know that we know what we know, and to know that we do
not know what we do not know, that is true knowledge."

—NICOLAUS COPERNICUS

As you can imagine, the holidays were a tough time for me the
year my villain fired me. It seemed like the entire world had
shut down and no one wanted to hear from me. Having spent the
majority of my career in corporate America, I was used to a very linear and clear path. Going to work for yourself is exactly the opposite.
Being an entrepreneur is much more like an EKG readout. There are
enormous highs and then quick dips, and then more highs and some
major lows when you least expect them.

When you're first on your own, the next step and the next day are
not clear, but you have to move forward and take action to discover
what your next path is. The key is to move forward, even when you
aren't exactly sure where you're headed.

While my new reality brought some major challenges, I remembered some of the things I learned in corporate America that were
useful to me. I learned in corporate sales, for example, that the
trajectory of a salesperson is not linear. In fact, as I considered the

trajectories of the successful sellers on my old team, I realized that most had a very difficult first year. They were busy establishing contacts, filling their pipelines, and refining their pitches.

This first year was typically the year they closed the least number of deals as they practiced their pitches and gained confidence in their sales abilities. If done right, however, this first year would set up their second for major success! They had closed some small deals and were ready to start going after bigger asks. The whole thing was a progression.

Now I was navigating in unchartered waters, and I was building a business with no previous history. I was operating in the dark. What would *my* trajectory look like? I couldn't afford to wait a year to make money—I was a single mom with bills to pay. I needed to move fast. I needed to figure out some way to take what I had learned in my corporate sales career to a new arena. The pressure to generate revenue got me laser focused.

When I first decided to go to work for myself, I knew I would need to create products that I could sell—creating a growing business in the process. But what kinds of products? After much thought and research, the answer became crystal clear. My very first product would be a book. Of course, I had never written a book before, and I had no idea where to start. So, I did what anyone does when they want to figure out how to do something new.

I googled it.

When I googled "how to write a book," I found some really good advice: Just start writing. Don't overcomplicate things.

I quickly learned that you don't need some fancy strategy to write a book; you just need words on paper—hopefully, *good* words. Done. I wrote and wrote and wrote. Every day I set aside time to write, and then I wrote some more.

Once I had a book's worth of content, I needed someone who could take my writing to the next level. I was *not* a professional writer, after all. I googled that and discovered that I needed to get an editor—someone who specializes in making book manuscripts better.

Done. One more thing: I wanted to name my book *Confidence Creator,* but I wasn't sure if I could legally use that title. Off to Google again! I learned that titles cannot be copyrighted, unlike the contents of the book. Problem solved and on to the next one.

Confidence Creator was mine.

As I mentioned earlier, that's when others' self-limiting beliefs showed up, threatening to derail my very first product. Friends told me the name seemed too aggressive and would make me look like I was full of myself. It's not easy when those who love you believe they are helping you when in fact they are attempting to extinguish your dreams. I had just left a career in which I was forced to accept others' self-limiting beliefs. I was the boss now, so I didn't need to check in with anyone in order to make a decision. Those days were over—done and buried.

I thanked everyone for their concerns, handed their self-limiting beliefs back to them, and moved forward with my decision. I asked myself what I thought about the title, and I liked it. To me, it said that everyone can be their own confidence creator, and I loved the idea of that. On to the next one.

Writing a book is just one-half of the process. Once you write it, you've got to publish it. If you've decided to self-publish your book, then you're taking on a lot of work and potential headaches. For me, the self-publishing headaches began early and hit often. I missed my deadlines countless times because I didn't know what printer to use or how many copies to print or if I should sign an exclusive with Amazon. The decisions were fast and furious. Some I chose correctly and some I did not. Having no experience in this field was painful.

The printer missed our agreed deadline three times, and things got so tense that I refused to pay their invoices. I was promising people advance copies of my hardcover but had to deliver paperbacks because the printer prioritized other jobs over mine. This may not sound like a dealbreaker. But as a self-published author and a rookie, you need to appear as professional as others, and I was not. I had zero clout in this industry. I was a beginner, and I was treated as such. This was beyond frustrating, but I knew I had to take action to get the printer to uphold their part of the bargain.

As always, when I called, I asked to be connected directly to the head of the company. I didn't care that I was a small fish in a big pond, I needed to be heard and I needed the games to end. I eventually got the president's cell phone, and we were able to reach an agreement. He would pay for the first run and overnight copies to me in NYC the next day in time for my press appearances. Problem solved.

Not quite.

The case of books arrived, and I was so grateful that things had finally come together. I opened the box and saw that the glossy black cover I had ordered wasn't a part of my book. Instead, I was looking at matte black covers—a difference like night and day. I had spent hours in bookstores looking at covers. I decided on a glossy black cover for my book because I could see that it would really stand out. To say I was upset doesn't even begin to communicate the disappointment I was feeling. Yet again I had been blown off. I felt as though I was being dismissed and taken advantage of, and it was not a good feeling.

It was, however, a familiar one.

This time I called the president's cell, and the call didn't go well at all.

I asked him how it was possible that yet again my order was disregarded—I had the order in my hand and it stated glossy covers, not matte. He told me that he was the one who ordered them because he never sees glossy covers and assumed I wanted matte. I asked what he was going to do to rectify the situation, and I didn't like his answer. I told him we were going to circle back on this open issue, but I had meetings to get to and I would think of a fair resolution.

Before I got back to him, I researched the amount of money I still owed his company and decided not paying the balance would be fair. Of course, bringing value to a negotiation and ensuring both parties leave feeling good about it is key to a successful negotiation. So when I called back, I told him the amount of press that I was going to do and the amount of support I could give him and how much I would promote his business. I had to make him want to make me happy. I shared with him my goal of creating a series of books and how I could partner with him again in a few months. I had to get him to see me as more than a beginner with one small project. Through three very difficult calls, we agreed that I would promote his business and use him again and recommend him if he would do the right thing and take care of my outstanding balance. We had finally agreed.

Sometimes when we're struggling and frustrated, we can be quick to blow up and react. By waiting just a bit—buying some time and calming down—we can operate much more successfully. By preparing for the call, accessing information, and doing some research, I put myself in a position in which I was operating with confidence. Arm yourself with information, give yourself some time, write down your notes, and go into the call coming from a place of strength, and that is how the other person will treat you.

One headache down, but there were more to go.

I next had to figure out how I was going to ship hundreds of books out to influencers and media while identifying friends with connections who could help me. The list of things to do was massive, and at each turn some problem or unexpected challenge arose. I see why people don't self-publish, but I also feel very proud having gone through it. And I no longer feel like a beginner.

If you've been dreaming of writing your own book, start by mocking up a fake book with your name on it, and keep it front and center so you see it every day! Here are some specific things you can do today to change your situation for tomorrow:

1. **Set goals.** If you are unhappy with where you are, you need to identify where it is that you want to go. Once you have your goal, you must write it down. Having a goal without a timeline is only a dream, so now you must give yourself a date by which you want to reach your goal. Next, set reminders and employ an accountability buddy to help you stay committed along the

way. Finding someone who encourages you and helps you along the way is critical to success.

2. **Failing to plan is planning to fail.** We can have the best intentions and the loudest cheerleaders, but if we don't have a road map on how to get where we want to go, we will never find our way. Creating a plan for how to get where we are going—with timelines and mini goals along the way—will help us stay focused and on track. There is nothing wrong with recruiting someone who has accomplished what you want to do to help you devise the best plan possible for you and hold you accountable.

3. **Focus on your accomplishments.** To try something new, we need to tap into our own individual strengths. Keeping a log of your proudest accomplishments and adding to it each day will help you focus on the fact that you can achieve goals and do something you were once afraid to try.

4. **Fear is a liar.** Realizing that fear is a liar, and that it is only our mind that creates and limits us every day, is extremely empowering. Anytime I am feeling afraid of something, I challenge myself to run through it and grow. Each day you challenge yourself to face a fear, you will become stronger. This initiative can be as simple as speaking up in a meeting, introducing yourself to a stranger, or deciding not to apologize at work anymore. Face one small fear head-on each day and watch how quickly you grow from it.

5. **Stay so focused on solutions that obstacles don't get in your way.** Obstacles are simply roadblocks that you will eventually overcome. Just because someone else couldn't doesn't mean *you* can't. There is always a solution.

Deciding to look at failure in a new light will propel you forward instead of pulling you back and keeping you stuck in the mud. There is one thing that I know for sure: taking action, trying new things, meeting new people, and running faster when I feel fear guarantees that I will grow.

And, as I grow, I gain strength and I gain clarity. I am no longer a beginner when it comes to writing a book. Everyone starts as a beginner.

KEY TAKEAWAY

Successful people don't always know the how, but they bet on themselves to figure it out along the way. This was the knowledge I was searching for my whole life.

I would love to hear your story and answer your questions!
To continue the conversation, join me wherever you are:

Twitter @_heathermonahan using #BAK
Instagram @heathermonahan using #confidencecreator
Linkedin @theheathermonahan using #overcomeyourvillains

CHAPTER 20

Identify Your Frenemy
and Take Action

"To attain knowledge, add things every day.
To attain wisdom, remove things every day."

—LAO TZU

While my work life was nothing short of shocking and unpredictable after I was fired, there also were some moments with my son that were pretty surprising—in a good way. So often we see on social media only the wins others have. Of course, this is often an illusion—you never really know what's going on in someone else's personal life. Most people on social media tend to share only the good stuff while avoiding the bad.

When my son, Dylan, was preparing for his final year in elementary school, he decided he wanted to run for school president. Dylan had run for class president in previous years and had won each time. The beautiful thing about success at any age is that it sets the tone for what you expect. Since he had won every other time he ran, he expected to win again this time—even though this was an election that every student at his school would vote in, not just his class. An object in motion remains in motion, and he believed wholeheartedly that he was heading for that title.

Dylan and I loved to work on his speeches and posters—it was fun for us to do together. For this campaign, we came up with the idea of DJ Khaled's "Another One"—since Dylan had won the past elections, the campaign would mean he would keep his positive momentum and win another one. DJ Khaled is a popular artist all of the kids knew, so it felt like a good fit, and he knew the kids would like it. The day came for all of the kids to submit their speeches and their campaign boards to the pastor who was the head of the election. Dylan's was accepted, and he was excited to deliver his speech the following week.

The week of the election, I received a call from the head of the election. He told me that, even though he had accepted Dylan's campaign board and speech, it had been brought to his attention that both were inappropriate for school. One of the moms of another student told him that DJ Khaled was misogynistic. She demanded that the campaign board be taken down and Dylan kicked out of the election.

Hmm . . . something was not sitting quite right with me.

Here's one thing I have learned in life that has served me very well: asking questions and remaining as calm as possible will help you get through even the most difficult situations. Another thing I know is that there aren't many situations that upset me as much as someone attacking my child. This was not going to be easy, but I had one clear goal in my mind: keep Dylan in that election, keep the board up, and not let haters get in the way of kids having fun.

My first question was, "I am confused. Didn't you accept his speech and campaign board already? Why would you be making changes now after you had accepted it? Who is the person who complained?"

Leading with "I am confused" is a great tactic to address a challenging situation.

I could tell the pastor was frustrated and was being forced to do this. He knew he had approved the speech and campaign board, and he didn't have a problem with them. The problem was the person who was complaining wanted Dylan out of the race. The pastor didn't feel it was appropriate to share the person's name with me, but at that very moment, I had a strong hunch who the mom was. I told the pastor that it must be the mother of another candidate, and he didn't have to tell me her name—I already knew. Then I let him know that I was a women's empowerment advocate and that there was nothing misogynistic about Dylan's board or campaign. He reiterated that he could not condone it, that the board had to come down, and Dylan's speech had to go.

I had a solution. I told him I knew he was stuck between a rock and a hard place. He had already accepted the campaign poster and speech, and just days before the election, he had a parent demanding that my son be disqualified. It was a difficult spot, and I wanted him to know I had empathy for him. But I also wanted him to know that I would not be bulldozed, and neither would my son.

"I have a solution for you," I told the pastor. "Your issue is the DJ Khaled reference, so I will come down to the school this afternoon and place tape over the word *one*. Then the board would simply read, 'Another. Dylan for President.' That will take DJ Khaled out of the picture entirely and allow Dylan to remain in the election."

Well, the pastor hadn't been prepared for that response, and he sounded very nervous. I was committed to finding a solution, one that allowed Dylan to remain in the election. The week became a nightmare. Things got very tense at school, and Dylan was told he needed to come up with a new speech two days before the election. It's crazy the extent that some people will go to win something or prop up their child. I knew that this situation was going to be a lesson for Dylan, and I wanted the lesson to be to never give up because there is always a solution. Never back down—instead, stand up for yourself when someone tries to intimidate or bully you.

The next day at school, I was lamenting to a teacher about the drama, and I asked her if she had any suggestions for my son. He had only a day to write and memorize a new speech, and I wasn't in the best, most positive mindset at that moment. She laughed and suggested I call the speaking coach everyone else in the school used.

What? I had no idea there was a kid's speaking coach, and no idea that everyone was using this person to help their kids. It's so funny when you find out what really goes on behind the scenes.

I grabbed the coach's number and ran to my car to call her. I told her exactly what had happened at school, and she felt badly about it. She agreed to stay late that night to work with Dylan. By this time, Dylan's heart was no longer into running for president because he couldn't do his funny DJ Khaled impersonation and bring his personality to his speech.

When your confidence is low, it makes a big difference to see others investing in you. So I invested in the coach, and then—after he trained an hour a and half with this woman—we came in and became his mock audience. Dylan had been told to remove humor and play it safe. And, given the angry parent who had it out for Dylan, I didn't want to give any reason for further drama. So Dylan's speech was rather dry. But what that coach did in that hour and a half was give Dylan hope again. She got him to shine his light a little more than before. She told him she wanted him to own his little quirks and be himself with his smile. Even though he couldn't use his jokes, he could still use his voice and his body and his movements. She believed in him, which elevated his confidence.

So many great things happened during the course of this experience. Dylan learned that, when you're faced with adversity, look for a solution because there always is one. He also learned that investing in yourself pays dividends and enlisting an expert will advance you quickly. He wasn't over the moon about his new speech, but his smile was back, and he was going to give his speech. I couldn't have been prouder of him.

He had twenty-four hours to rewrite it and give it his best with the added restrictions. When it came time to deliver it and make his appeal to his schoolmates, he got up there and gave it his best. He fully embraced his smile and the uniqueness of himself.

He lost the election to a boy no one had thought would win, but he learned a valuable lesson: sometimes just showing up is the win. It says that you can try to hold me back, but I will still show up as me. That is the ultimate win.

The boy whose mother had probably complained about Dylan became distant and cold to my son after both kids lost. This went on for a while, and we asked Dylan to ignore the other boy and not feed into the drama, hoping it would go away. This led us to another amazing lesson and experience.

A month after the election, the entire class was invited to a girl's birthday party at her home. It was the first nighttime birthday party for Dylan, where parents dropped off their kids and didn't stay, which was a big deal—for Dylan and me. The kids were so excited!

Later that evening, an hour before pickup, I got a call from Dylan. He was very upset, and I could hear his tears. He told me that the same boy had made up a story that Dylan said a swear word, and that boy had gone to the birthday girl's mother to tell her. He insisted that he hadn't said a swear word and that he couldn't believe this boy was making this story up. I asked if he wanted me to come and get him, and he said no. I asked what he wanted to do. He told me he was going to walk in and tell the mom the truth that he didn't swear. Then his best friend grabbed the phone and told me he was there—he saw the whole thing, and he was going in with Dylan because he didn't want him to go alone.

I thanked Dylan's friend for being such a stand-up young man. The two boys went in together and told the mom what had really happened.

Dylan learned an amazing lesson that day. He learned to stand up for himself and to speak his truth even though it wasn't easy. He also learned that doing it with a best friend who has your back makes it so much better. Getting to watch that experience unfold from my couch that night brought me to tears. Surrounding yourself with people who have your back is *everything*, and it can be the difference maker in finding the confidence to speak your truth.

I knew that while this issue was ongoing with the other boy, I needed to focus on Dylan staying positive. I made a few changes in his routine. Every night at bedtime I would ask him to tell me three things he was grateful for, and I wrote them down for him in his notebook. Then I asked him who he loved. He would tell me all of the people he loved, and I would remind him of the most important one: *himself*. He got in the habit of saying he loved himself and not laughing anymore; it just felt normal to him. Each morning, I would ask him what he was looking forward to that day. Creating a positive outlook is done through action steps, which anyone can learn at any age.

A couple of months later, Dylan had to wear jeans to school for a class picture. When you are divorced, sometimes there are some clothes at one house and not at the other. We couldn't find any jeans, so I had to put Dylan in a pair of jeans that were two sizes too big for him. They did not look good. He knew they didn't look good, but he needed to go to school. When he came home, I asked about his day and he said, "Well, my best friend had a great day."

"What do you mean?" He said that his best friend was calling Dylan "Farmer Dylan" all day, making fun of his jeans. I laughed and Dylan laughed while telling me the story. I asked him what he did when he made fun of his jeans.

"The only thing you can do when your best friend is crushing you for your awful jeans: I pulled them up as high as I could and walked around like a farmer. At least that gave everyone a laugh."

I was so happy to see that Dylan knew the difference between joking around with those we care about versus doing something malicious to hurt others. Life certainly isn't perfect, but it's these moments that make me so grateful.

Character is built in these moments. Growth happens when you are faced with adversity. How will you approach it?

KEY TAKEAWAY

Difficult situations build character and create resilience for the future. Using the expression "I am confused" is a phenomenal tactic to prompt others to explain themselves and diffuse a situation. Giving our kids the knowledge they need to handle challenging moments in their lives empowers them to take on and solve these challenges themselves.

I would love to hear your story and answer your questions!
To continue the conversation, join me wherever you are:

Twitter @_heathermonahan using #BAK
Instagram @heathermonahan using #confidencecreator
Linkedin @theheathermonahan using #overcomeyourvillains

CHAPTER 21

Put It Out to the Universe and Success Will Find You

"If knowledge is not put into practice,
it does not benefit one."

—MUHAMMAD TAHIR-UL-QADRI

I have traveled all over the country, taking every opportunity I can get to share my message with others. Some trips are fantastic, and others not so much, but you never know what ripple effect a trip or a meeting can have, and that's why I *always* go. Flying to LA for me is never easy, as I live in Miami and can't sleep on planes. It also means more time away from my little boy.

When I heard that I was booked for *Headline News* on CNN *and* for the Maria Menounos show on Sirius, I was beyond ecstatic. Holy cow! This was huge. This could be the break I needed to really get my new career off and running. At this point, I had no idea what I was doing when it came to promoting myself. I was literally throwing everything and anything against the wall, hoping something would stick. Yes, that was my strategy, and I am proud of it!

To say I was nervous is an understatement. Maria is one of those people whom I had put on a pedestal. She is gorgeous, articulate, successful, and in my mind, she was on another level I couldn't imagine.

I found out I had to go to her house to do the interview. Yikes, that scared me even more! The idea of rolling into her mansion trying to play it cool didn't sit well with me. This whole new world seemed scary, and part of me missed the comfort of sitting in an office where I knew what to expect. To get comfortable with this new situation, I knew I needed to push myself into the uncomfortable so much that it would begin to feel normal. Here we go.

When I get nervous, I move fast, act cold, and clench my teeth. Not a good look. That was how this beautiful morning started at the hotel. I was in a rush to get ready and wanted to look my best. I felt like a fraud. Who was I going to this woman's home? This whole thing seemed surreal.

I called an Uber and went out in front of the hotel, awaiting its arrival. I waited. And waited some more. No car, no nothing.

Now I panicked. I can't be late for the woman I have on a pedestal. I called a cab, and yes, a crappy little cab picked me up. I begged him to speed. We went into the gates of her amazing home, and I screeched up in my crappy little cab. That was exactly how I felt: crappy, small.

I jumped out of the cab, realizing I was a few minutes late. Out came the assistant to get me, and before I could even mutter a word, I saw Maria. She was sitting on a beautiful swing surrounded by trees and flowers, and her hair and makeup were perfect. She called my name and announced that she loved my book and had already read it twice. I was in shock. This was crazy! She then told me to go into the theater room to wait and they would call for me when they were ready.

This is when you do the happy dance! Not only had she read my book, she loved it! Her theater room was gorgeous, and I was snapping pics like a tourist. Her cohost, Jenni Pulos, came in to sit and talk with me. I didn't know her, but she was hilarious, and she quickly put me at ease. Then an assistant walked us into Maria's studio. Not just a spare bedroom but a full-blown studio attached to her house.

How amazing is this? I imagined how many years she had worked to reach this level of success.

We sat down and I could feel myself shaking. That's when Maria told me about how she had been bullied for a good portion of her career, but she hadn't realized it until she read *Confidence Creator*. This shocked me.

I saw her as beautiful and confident, and I was surprised to hear from her that she wasn't confident and had allowed producers to bully her and had learned to laugh it off. She didn't want to upset them because she feared losing her job. The more real she was with me, the more the pedestal began to disappear and the more I felt that we were so much alike. That was a serious transition moment for me. One woman's honesty allowed me to see that, no matter what something looks like on the outside, we never have any idea what is really going on inside.

The show went really well, and I was beyond grateful for learning that pedestals didn't have a place in my life any longer. Jenni and Maria walked me outside, and Maria told me she wanted to help me and get the book out to the world. "How can I help?" she asked.

"Do you know Reese Witherspoon?" I inquired. Of course, I asked her for one specific thing, because if you don't ask, you don't get.

"No, but why do you ask?"

I explained that Reese not only had one of the largest book clubs in the country, but she also had a woman-led film production company that creates movies based on female-authored books.

She stood there for a moment and said, "I wish I knew her. If anything comes up and I can think of a way, I will reach out to you. Here is my cell—keep me updated."

She then asked me one more thing: "As far as book sales go, what has worked best for you so far?"

I shared with her that the James Altucher podcast had the biggest impact, and I asked her if she wanted me to connect her to the producer to get her on. She was so excited and said *yes*. I was, of course, happy to make the introduction for her.

Maria's assistant, Ashley, walked me out of the gates to get the Uber. She shared with me that she, too, had read my book and would love to talk when I had time. I gave her my cell, and she gave me hers. Having the gatekeeper's info is always so important. It was a humbling experience that opened my eyes to see how I could help Maria to do something just as she was trying to help me. I felt good.

The next day I was still in LA, sitting in a waiting room pumping myself up in my mind because I was about to go into a first meeting with Steve Harvey's producer to pitch myself for his show. My phone rang and it was Maria. This is crazy. She told me to sit down because she had just gotten a phone call from Reese Witherspoon who asked Maria if she could appear on her podcast next Friday.

This is not normal. I can tell you that in my twenty years in corporate America, I had zero experiences like this—*zero*. If less than zero is a number, then that too. I was dumbfounded. Maria felt the same way and couldn't believe this just happened. She said she had the chills. Maria asked me to overnight books to her assistant, personally signed for each person who would be there, and she would guarantee to pitch me and the book to them. Then she let me know she was jumping on a flight and to please text her and remind her next Friday.

I was on high alert. For some reason, every time I launched social media or turned on the TV, something about Reese Witherspoon would come up. What the heck was going on? Did I really speak something into the universe and suddenly it was showing up? Was I becoming a hippie? Do things like this really happen? Where has this power been my whole life?

I flew home to Miami and reached out to Maria's assistant, Ashley. She was so excited for me and promised to get the books to Maria so she would have them to give to Reese and her team. I overnighted three books to Ashley and wrote a personal note in each one. One was for Reese (and I gave her my cell), one was for her podcast cohost, and one was for the president of Hello Sunshine. One of them would surely read it! Ashley received the books and got them to Maria—and then we waited.

That next Friday, I could barely focus on any meeting that I had. I was constantly checking the time on my phone. When it hit noon, I shot Maria a text asking her to please pitch the book to Reese and thank you so much! Then crickets.

I was so nervous! I tend to get very excited about things, and then, if they don't happen, I can get pretty bummed out. I had a great feeling about this and kept my fingers crossed. I spent the day going to venues in Miami where I had pitched myself to speak—following up, securing details, and asking if they would help me to promote the event and the book.

By the time 10:00 p.m. rolled around, I was beyond upset. In my mind, I had created a story that Maria probably had bad news for me, so she didn't want to reach out. Ugh. I sat on my couch and felt so deflated. Then I got a voice note from Maria. She said she had been slammed all day and hadn't had a chance to follow up with me, but it went amazing. She told them how much she loved the book, and they said they would read it. Maria also explained that she didn't have plans to see Reese again but thought that the one meeting was enough to get them interested in reading the book and reaching out to me. I was so grateful.

This experience really opened my eyes to the possibility of manifesting and putting something out to the universe. I had *never* had an experience like this when I was in corporate America, and I was open-minded to the idea that now things might be different for me. Just maybe, since I was pursuing my passion and stepping into my power and helping others, the universe was responding and giving me an assist.

It was something I would consider for quite some time to come.

KEY TAKEAWAY

No matter how crazy your ideas or dreams may seem to you right now, writing them down, reading them in the present tense, feeling what it feels like to achieve them, and sharing them with others will open up a world of opportunity to set you on the path to achievement.

I would love to hear your story and answer your questions! To continue the conversation, join me wherever you are:

Twitter @_heathermonahan using #BAK
Instagram @heathermonahan using #confidencecreator
Linkedin @theheathermonahan using #overcomeyourvillains

CHAPTER 22

Show Up As the Real You

> "Unless we learn to know ourselves,
> we run the danger of destroying ourselves."
>
> —JA A. JAHANNES

One of my former employees reached out to me about a WNBA women's empowerment event coming to the MGM Grand Hotel in Las Vegas. He wanted to pitch me as a speaker for the event. After explaining everything to me, I sent him a reel and talking points, and the following week I heard from the woman in charge. She wanted to read my book first, which always happens and can be frustrating while I wait for a reaction. But I sent her a copy, waited two weeks, and then called her again. I am constantly putting notes in my computer calendar to ensure I don't forget to follow up. Follow-up is always on *us* and never on the other party.

I reached back out to her, and she told me she loved the book. I was focused on booking new speaking opportunities, and I knew this would be a good one for me to build my visibility and my brand. I asked for the opportunity and she agreed but explained she couldn't pay speaking fees, only travel. I accepted. I knew I had to take some large stages with major brands like the WNBA in order to get to the next level, so I was more than willing to do it. I was really excited for the opportunity, and I was super appreciative for this past employee of mine to think of me.

It was kind of funny because, a couple months earlier, he had been looking for a new opportunity and had reached out to me. He wanted me to call someone I knew to recommend him for the job. I did it immediately and then forgot about it. Apparently, he hadn't forgotten. The more acts of kindness you do, the more kindness is thrust upon you.

One of my good friends, Danielle, saw a post about my trip and called me to ask if I wanted to have dinner the night of my birthday since I was going to be in Vegas and she was going to be there as well. I was so excited! No one had said anything to me about my birthday because I had agreed to travel that day and the WNBA event was the following day. I felt so happy to know that I had a wingwoman waiting for me when I landed and was not going to be alone on my special day.

I took off for Vegas the morning of my birthday and hadn't heard from my son or my fiancé at the time. I was feeling hurt. I posted on social media that it was my birthday, and I received so many amazing notes and comments supporting me. That helped me take a down moment and turn it into something good. I landed, and there was a text and a voicemail from my son. I was suddenly feeling much better.

I made my way into the MGM lobby to check into my room, and there was a massive Vegas-style line waiting for me. If you haven't spent much time in Vegas, the hotel check-in lines are reminiscent of a ninety-nine-cent all-you-can-eat buffet. They're massive.

I saw there was no one in the VIP line so I decided to go for it. I took the split-second chance that, yes, I might be kicked out of the line, but the worst that would happen is I would be redirected to the end of the long line. But the best that could happen is I could check in immediately instead of waiting in the other line for forty minutes.

I held my head high and smiled big as I ran up to VIP, telling the woman at the counter how excited I was to be there on my birthday! She was so happy for me and got caught up asking me about my birthday and what I was going to do that night. Then I told her I was speaking for the MGM and WNBA the next day.

"Oh, you are a speaker—amazing! Okay, let's go ahead and get you taken care of."

This woman was sweet. I really wasn't a VIP, and she may have known it, but taking the chance and going to the window with excitement and sharing my story allowed her to engage with me and make the decision to help me. This was an epic birthday win. Whenever you see an opportunity, go for it. What's the worst that can happen?

I got to the room fast, and it was already time to get ready to go meet Danielle for drinks before dinner. I hadn't heard from my fiancé yet, however, and now I was mad. He was the person who always made birthdays special for everyone. He loved birthdays and celebrating them more than anyone I had ever met. Except for this one. He had flown that day from Boston to Miami with his son, returning from a baseball trip for school. I finally got a text that read, "Happy Birthday! Just getting home—hope you're having a great day and hope you have a great time tonight. Love you. Not feeling well so going to bed."

Yikes. When I would be disappointed, I used to let it affect me a lot. I have learned, however, that I cannot allow others' behaviors to affect me. I have to learn how to observe their behavior and not let it take me on a downward spiral. I didn't like that he was so busy that he didn't remember my birthday until the end of his day, but I wasn't going to let it ruin *my* day. Instead, I was going to decide to enjoy being with my girlfriend and revel in the fact that I was on the eve of speaking for the WNBA, which was mind-blowing!

Danielle and I had a great dinner. We toasted my birthday and I kicked off my forty-fourth year in Vegas. How bad is life?

The next morning, my phone ringing woke me up. It was my fiancé calling me to check how my night was. Here's what I know about me: I can be emotional, I can get angry, and when these things happen, I don't show up as the best me. Knowing this, I have learned to create boundaries on any day that I am going to speak. I told him we had a great dinner. But I reminded him I was speaking for the WNBA event that afternoon and needed to get in the zone. That meant I needed him to respect that I needed my space and peace to do it. I let him know I would call him after I was done.

Claiming the space I need when I need it is the difference between doing an okay job and killing it. I know what I need, and I am at a place in my life where I let others know too. This is how to show up as your best you. Ask for what you want, and you will get it.

It was time for me to get dressed. Since I was only going to be there for one night and one day, I didn't pack much. I pulled out my outfit: white blazer, black bodysuit, and black jeans. Everything was good except one thing: I had packed the wrong black jeans—the *ripped* black jeans. And not just ripped—the knees were absolutely *shredded*.

OMG. After all of these years in corporate America, there was no way I could walk out on a stage in a pair of ripped black jeans. There wasn't enough time to go and find something else, so I put the outfit on. I took pictures of me in the mirror and sent them to my friends. I was panicked. This wasn't the plan.

That is when I remembered they were *my* jeans.

They weren't the ones I planned to wear, but they were still mine. They were jeans that I wore. I had never worn ripped jeans before to a speech, but I do wear ripped jeans in my life. I wasn't going to wait for the replies from my friends. I looked good and these were *my* jeans. I would rather show up as *me*. I was going.

That was a *massive* moment for me. Making the decision to show up as me, knowing that people might not like it but going anyway, was a breakthrough confidence-building moment.

As the Uber took me down the Strip, we passed by the MGM Grand, and I saw my event on the marquis. *What?* No, my name wasn't up there, but it was my event!

I texted Danielle immediately to record it when she came to the event, and I made the Uber driver make a U-turn and go around so I could get pictures. I thought to myself, "Who would have imagined a few months earlier that I'd be fired, but now I would be driving down the Las Vegas Strip and seeing a marquis promoting *my* event?" How things had changed in just a few months.

> While that woman thought she fired me
> that day, what she didn't realize was
> she could never take the fire within me.

Life truly holds so many surprises for you when you decide to fire your villains and step into your superpower. Things were shaping up in ways I could have never imagined. *So* much better than I had ever imagined. When everything is uncertain, anything is possible.

After my meeting, I made it to the event, which was being promoted everywhere. There are not words to describe what it feels like the first time you see something you are doing in lights on the Vegas Strip. Why did I play it small for so long? That was the question that popped into my head.

I walked into the event, wondering what the response would be to my outfit and still not knowing if this was going to work. I was immediately greeted by the team, and they were fantastic. I saw that the Girl Scouts of America were there and got the chance to speak to many of them—it was fantastic. I began to feel at ease surrounded by so many positive people who weren't judging me for my clothes the way I used to feel at the last company I worked for. Instead, people were excited to see me and grateful I was there.

The speakers were called to the front and I headed up. I saw Danielle in the audience—it always makes me feel great seeing a familiar face and being supported. When we finished, we were asked to stand in a line for the audience to have access to us, and that is when two beautiful young women rushed up to me to tell me they loved my style and my outfit and wished they had the confidence I did to dress as who they really were.

Showing up as the real me always pays dividends. Dress for you.
Be you. Show up for you. And watch how everything else begins to
take off!

Ripped jeans and all. ☺

That next morning, I packed up to catch my flight home. I stood
on the Strip looking around and feeling so proud. That is when I
caught the image on the hotel across from me. It was a huge marquis
promoting Jennifer Lopez's show with her face and her name up in
lights. I admired the image and thought to myself, I am going to have
my face and my name up there someday. If she can do it, why can't
I? The next time I come back for an event in Vegas, I am going next
level, and it will be my face and my name. I can literally envision that
happening, so it will.

See yourself at that next level, feel what it feels like to be there, and
put it out to the universe. Why not me? And why not you?

KEY TAKEAWAY

The most important person you are ever going to get to know
is the one staring back at you in the mirror. As you begin to
know the real you, you will be able to own who you really are.
Doing this will make you the most powerful version of yourself,
which will allow you to reach goals that were formerly out of
your grasp.

I would love to hear your story and answer your questions!
To continue the conversation, join me wherever you are:

Twitter @_heathermonahan using #BAK
Instagram @heathermonahan using #confidencecreator
Linkedin @theheathermonahan using #overcomeyourvillains

CHAPTER 23

Just Think *Bigger*!

"A true teacher would never tell you what to do.
But he would give you the knowledge with which you
could decide what would be best for you to do."

—CHRISTOPHER PIKE

Who are the people you spend your time with? Have you done an audit of these coworkers, friends, and family? Are they holding you back—getting in the way of you achieving your goals—or catapulting you forward? What would it take for you to leave behind the people who are standing in your way and get you to go bigger?

In the old days, when I worked for a large corporation, my friends and I would regularly take vacations to the Florida Keys or Palm Beach. We could easily reach either by car, and there were fabulous places to stay that made you feel like you were on your own personal island. We would usually go somewhere amazing during the major breaks when the kids were off of school—Labor Day, President's Day, spring break, and the rest.

That all changed when I became my own boss.

As an entrepreneur with unpredictable and erratic income my first year, this didn't seem to be the way I could live any longer. I had a talk with my son, Dylan, and let him know we wouldn't be going on so many trips as I focused on building my company. I believe he understood as this was our new life, but I wonder if *I* really did. Each time I would be asked to go on the next trip with my friends, I would politely decline and feel bummed out that Dylan and I were missing out on those amazing trips.

While I realize these are first-world problems, when your life has been one way for twenty years, it takes a bit of adjusting. I also realized I didn't really want to adjust—I needed to find a way to accelerate revenues faster, and I hadn't been able to find that solution quite yet. I knew it would be there; I just had to be patient, persistent, and find it. Revenue fixes all problems.

On Labor Day, I received the same ask—to go to the Breakers in Palm Beach for the weekend with my friends and their families. I automatically declined, as I had been doing for some time, when I suddenly remembered that my son was going on a trip with his father over the holiday weekend. So I would be able to stay in my girlfriend's room instead of having to pay for my own. The cost would be minimal, and I would have a much-needed opportunity to get out of the house and have a fun day and night with my friends!

I was *in*.

I drove to Palm Beach and was blown away by the massive hotel and all the activities for kids. It had been over a year since I had last been there. While I never missed my old job, I sure missed my old guaranteed paycheck. I met up with my friends, and we all headed to the pool so their kids could swim and we could eat lunch.

Janine and Bobby had been married for the past decade and had helped see me through all my highs and lows. They had two little kids who were adorable and consumed with the pool. When your kids are young, you have to play the divide-and-conquer game to ensure that one adult is always on watch—keeping your little ones from slipping underwater. Janine and I had been talking for a while when her husband, Bobby, asked for her to switch. That's when Bobby asked me to go sit with him and get some lunch.

As soon as we sat down, he started with the questions. Bobby has been an entrepreneur forever. He gets excited talking about it and has enjoyed tremendous financial success, so for me he is a great person to speak with and learn from. Anytime I can talk to someone who has been where I am and has broken through, it inspires me to do the same.

Bobby asked me a lot of questions about what I had been doing and how it was going. I shared everything about my business, but then I added, "I just don't know if this is really going to work. I am definitely keeping the door open that I may just go back to media and take a similar job to my old one but with a better company."

Those last couple of sentences were part of my standard script. I had told only a few close friends and colleagues that I was starting my own company because I was so afraid I would fail. I figured it was better that I keep it quiet.

Bobby was floored. "What did you say? Did you just say that you came all of this way but you may still go back to a career you outgrew years ago? No. I am not letting you speak like that. In fact, you need to turn it around. You don't need to think smaller to keep yourself safe, you need to think bigger to make it work!"

Holy cow. I had never thought of it this way. I hadn't thought that the problem might be that I was trying to straddle my past and a train that was leaving the station. I had one leg anchored behind me and one trying to find a foothold ahead of me. There was no way I could stay in that place anymore—it wasn't physically possible.

I realized in that moment that if I was going to make this work, I had to go all in. Yes, I had written my book and I was building my business, but I still wasn't all in. I still had my eye on the dusty little path that would take me back to my old comfort zone in case things got too tough. I was still keeping a door open for a career that I should have closed the door on a decade earlier.

Yet again, fear had snuck into my mind and worked its dark magic on me. And the whole time I hadn't even realized it.

Bobby sat with me for more than an hour, giving me ideas on how I could go bigger.

I would say, "I'm booking some good shows and promoting the book."

He would counter with, "Fox News. Now that's *big*—think bigger. Only the biggest is what you should focus on now. No excuses."

"Well, I would, but I don't have an agent or a PR person, and I don't know anyone there."

"Ha! When you were in sales and you needed to get to a client, what would you do?"

"I would send a life-size cutout of myself, and I would show up and ask to see them. I would find someone we knew in common on social media and ask for an intro. Bottom line, I would always find a way."

Then Bobby went on to tell me that he had worked with Evel Knievel years ago. The lesson he learned from Evel was to never let any roadblock stop you. Evel's personal roadblock was that no one knew who he was early in his career. He didn't have a big name, and he didn't command a big audience. He decided the solution was to make himself seem as though he had a huge audience and bring that audience to Caesar's Palace in Las Vegas when they booked the date.

So Evel marched right into Caesar's Palace with no following, and he told them he would sell the hotel out with his show. He never even implied that it might not happen. He went all in on his vision, and guess what? He got the show. Had he said, "Listen—I'm not really sure how many people will show up, or how the show will go," we would never have heard about Evel Knievel.

Everyone starts as a beginner. Some stay there, and some retreat. But others—the successful ones—lean into the fear and claim their greatness.

Hearing all of this made me extremely excited and optimistic! I had been feeling down that I didn't have my old paycheck, and within an hour, I was raring to get back to work and get bigger and bolder!

Bobby asked me why I didn't have my books for sale in Costco. When I told him that it doesn't work like that because I was self-published, he laughed. "Excuse!" he exclaimed. "Let's do this—get a stack of your books and you and I will head to Costco. I'll film everything. We will cover one of their giant endcaps with your book, and we will record what other people say when they pick it up and look at it. What's the worst that can happen? What will happen is we will get footage of people loving your book and then trying to buy it. Costco is going to have to bring it in—how about that?"

Well, I hadn't thought about that kind of approach. I had been brainwashed in the conventional way of thinking, which was that self-published books are sold only on Amazon.

No more. No way. I am bigger than this.

Bobby wrapped up our chat with a great analogy: "It's like you're sitting on the side of a river looking in and saying 'I know if I jump in I can swim hard enough and fast enough to make it, but for some reason I haven't jumped in.' Realize *this* is the time to jump! Not next week, next month, or a year from now. A year from now, the current may pick up, and you won't be able to make it. Jump!"

Bobby knew I could do it, and I knew it too. No more excuses or waiting for someone else to do it for me. I am jumping—right now!

I left the Breakers that day overjoyed and anxious to go big and make major things happen in my business and my life. I was so excited. As soon as I got home, I put together an action plan—the steps I would take the very next morning. The emails I would send, people I would call, pitches I would send out, meetings I was going to set up. That next morning, I was ready to go big as an *entrepreneur*. No going back, no path to my old job.

I closed the door once and for all on the past and stepped through the door to my future.

This was a game changer.

After I finished my plan, I sent a thank-you email to Bobby and sat down to watch TV and rest up for the next day when I would put the plan into action. I turned on Netflix, and the movie *The Secret* caught my attention. I had heard of it but never seen it, so I sat down and watched. When it ended, I wrote down my main impressions from the film on a piece of paper—I still revisit them every day:

9/2/18

What you focus on is what you attract.
The Secret—the creative process:

1. Ask for what you want—let the universe know what you want.
2. Believe that it's already yours and have unwavering faith in what you cannot see. People don't know how they are going to do something; they just know that they will. There is zero room for doubt.
3. Receive—begin to feel the way you will once it arrives. Feeling good putting out that frequency of what you are wanting. You have to feel it to make it real.

Test drive the car you want, go to tour the house you want to buy, create the real feeling so it will be.
The universe likes speed—when you feel it, act!
Focus on what you *do* want, not on what you don't want. Visualize it, feel what it feels like, and stay in that feeling.

Here is my new manifesting statement that I am making real:
I'm so happy and grateful that I have sold over a million books and helped so many people. Now money flows freely and easily to me. I create and enjoy my life by shining my light!
Your wish is my command.
What will *you* manifest?

KEY TAKEAWAY

It is essential to have people in your life who are ahead of you. When you surround yourself with successful people, they will inspire you to push past your current limitations and allow you to see something much bigger in yourself that you hadn't previously thought of. Accessing knowledge from those who are light-years ahead of us is priceless.

I would love to hear your story and answer your questions! To continue the conversation, join me wherever you are:

Twitter @_heathermonahan using #BAK
Instagram @heathermonahan using #confidencecreator
Linkedin @theheathermonahan using #overcomeyourvillains

CHAPTER 24

Set Expectations Up Front

"Knowledge is power? No. Knowledge on its own is nothing,
but the application of useful knowledge, now that is powerful."

—ROB LIANO

At the end of 2018, as the holidays arrived, everything seemed to slow to a screeching halt. I decided I needed to circle back and create some new momentum. A friend of mine had connected me to a networking group in Miami, and I decided to reach back out to the woman in charge—Christina—to see if she wanted to do an event on confidence creation. Christina was quick to respond and wanted to schedule an event for the beginning of January.

It was the holiday season, so I wasn't worried when I didn't hear back from her after that. My son and I celebrated the New Year, and I sent an email to Christina, outlining what I was planning on doing at the event. I didn't hear back. I reached out again and got a note that I would hear from her soon.

The night of the event, just as I was getting ready to head out, Christina called.

She let me know she had been sick but was back and excited for our event. I asked if there was anything specific she wanted me to accomplish, and she said, "Just make sure you have an hour's worth of exercises for my people and it will be a success."

Hmm. I had never done exercises. That wasn't how I planned for this event to go, but I decided to roll with it anyway.

Okay. I had an hour to come up with some exercises. I was confident I could do it, thanks to a special way of thinking I learned from my good friend and former coworker Rafe. With intense deadlines and grueling travel schedules, we often found ourselves having to quickly create presentations or prepare for speeches or a variety of other things. Rafe coined the phrase, "Twenty-four hours is a lifetime." What he meant is that in twenty-four hours you can create or accomplish anything. Twenty-four hours is more than enough time to get *anything* done.

Knowing this is true because I had lived it for the last decade, I decided that an hour was plenty of time to create exercises. So, quit worrying about it and sit down and start writing.

I pulled out a blank sheet of paper and started thinking about what people tell me after I speak or after they read my book. I turned these points into exercises. I listened to myself, didn't ask anyone else what they thought, and I took that sheet of paper with me. I decided on twenty exercises, hoping that with three minutes devoted to each one, it would add up to the hour I needed. Let's go!

In some ways, I was very excited. I like the challenge of trying to create something new that can help others, and I couldn't wait to see what their feedback was.

The event was laid back, and I started with my regular keynote, which I have done so many times. It always puts me at ease. I could read the faces and see that the audience was engaged. I tightened up the talk to leave time for the exercises. Then we began. The audience had great questions and got to work right there in front of me. It was so powerful to see that this group wanted to improve and change their lives and that they loved the exercises. It was clear that this was a first step to overcoming their villains.

These exercises must have written answers:

1. List your villains, then answer these questions:
   How will you fire them?
   What is your deadline?
2. No more comparing yourself with others: Who are you unfollowing right now on social media?
3. How can you put that comparison to work for you? How can you reframe it to benefit you? If that person gets paid more than you, can you see that as more upside and potential for you to shoot for? Write down your new goals for yourself now that you see they can be obtained.
4. Thirty-day commitment to confidence: Who will be your accountability partner? Send the ask now.
5. What are your New Year claims? Put them out there. Speak them into existence. What is the biggest goal you are putting out to the universe?
6. What makes you feel scared? Not a burglar. What step do you want to take but you don't because you feel scared? Let's act on it now! Fear is a green light that means go. Fear is a liar! Even a small step counts—what small step can you take?
7. Who can you ask for help? Strong and confident people ask for help. Reach out with your ask now.
8. How will you invest in yourself? Sign up for a course? Listen to a podcast? Get a babysitter so you can go to the gym? Make the decision and do it. If you don't put yourself first, no one else will either.
9. Three things you are grateful for right now—write them down. Now do this every day. This truly changes the way you think and feel.
10. Rewrite the tape that plays in your head. Write the new tape now. Commit to reading it daily. *I am confident. I am doing this. I am smart. I am amazing*, and so on.

11. Leave yourself reminders. Put them in your phone now. Where else will you leave them? Write them on your shoes! I can and I will!

12. Find a picture of you when you were a baby or little child, and keep it in your wallet. The next time you speak negatively to yourself, hold that photo and stop yourself and change the conversation to encouragement. Speak to yourself the same way you would speak to a child.

13. No more apologies—for seven days you will not apologize. You will say "excuse me" or "thank you," but no more "I am sorry."

14. Share a win or a proud moment with the group or on social media. Celebrate you and your wins and watch everyone celebrate with you! When you do this, you inspire others to see what is possible for them too.

15. Identify your superpower and spend your time there. If you hate accounting, don't do accounting. Spend your time where you find your joy. This is the one life you have—live it for you!

16. How can you reframe your doubt? Write it down. Why would Harvard want me to speak? Why *wouldn't* Harvard want me to speak?

17. What action step can you take right now to move you toward your goal? Now do three more! It's a numbers game. The more times you try, the better your chances of succeeding.

18. Unique value proposition email—send it now. What is special or unique or different about me that makes me, me? Send this to ten people in your life and watch your confidence soar. This will help you to see your talents or skills that you take for granted but that others see massive value in.

19. What image of yourself will you use to keep top of mind what you are creating? Where you will be in thirty days? Find that pic and keep it everywhere. If you don't have a pic of you feeling your best, one that channels your inner Beyoncé, grab a

confident photo of her until you have become *your* most confident.

20. Draw out your thirty-day plan, each day represented by a square. Cross off each day as you go. Take notes for each day: what action steps you took, journal, gratitude, what showed up or happened. What is your theme song for when you reveal yourself? Start to feel it. You will begin to see that, during Week 2, amazing opportunities showed up that you didn't even know in Week 1 would occur. That makes you optimistic for what unknown fabulous event may happen the following week.

21. To think bigger, we need to surround ourselves with people who have done things we haven't done. Who can you tap right now? Think bigger! You were made for more!

22. Write a letter to the you from ten years ago—what advice would you give that person? Move faster, take bigger risks, bet on you, be kind to you. . . . Now, implement those things in your life today.

23. Saying no is your right and duty. *No* is also a complete sentence that does not need an explanation. Saying no gives you time back to spend on things *you* want to do. What do you need to say no to right now?

The best part about creating these exercises for the event was it opened my eyes to the need to put my ideas out to the world. In fact, I had been thinking about launching an online course to teach the steps to finding confidence at work and in life, but I hadn't done it yet. So many times I wanted to launch this course but felt too overwhelmed to get started.

As I stood there in that room, the framework for the course popped right into my mind—I could see it. Just then, a young woman walked up to me and introduced herself. Gabi was a twenty-year-old college student who loved my message and wanted to work with me. Now, this may sound negative, but college students have approached me a few times before, and when I let them know I couldn't afford to pay them yet, I would never hear back from them. I didn't realize it then, but this time was going to be different.

Gabi told me she would reach out to me the following week and she did. She agreed to work for me as an intern—simply to gain experience. We made an appointment for our first in-person meeting, and she showed up right on time. Not only that, but she was prepared. I was blown away.

I shared with Gabi that my number one priority, and what I wanted her to focus on, was launching my online course. In business, the best way to increase your income is to either raise your prices on existing products or services, or to increase your offerings. I didn't want to raise my prices, so I decided to increase my offerings. Adding a course to the mix seemed like an amazing idea.

We sat at my table with papers all over the place, and I showed Gabi how I wanted the course to flow. My plan was to first launch all of my videos, then follow up with worksheets and other products. Gabi told me that is not how they do it in school. Instead, first there's a welcome in which expectations are set, then the video, then the corresponding worksheet and Q&A, and only then the next video. I was grateful for Gabi's input. My expertise was the content, not the formatting. Her expertise was as a student who knew how courses were delivered most effectively. Having her different background and expertise helped me immensely. I also appreciated her enthusiasm: Gabi was genuinely excited about helping me create a great product.

Within forty-eight hours, Gabi sent me the course name and outline—no content up yet, but there was something for me to see. Also, that she made this happen in just two days opened my eyes to me doing it too. I had been procrastinating because I saw it as such a major undertaking, but Gabi was able to make a major dent in just a little bit of time. That's when I jumped in.

Within two weeks, we had the entire course done. We were both excited and proud. Momentum is an amazing thing. It takes one small thing to start moving, and suddenly it all seems possible, then probable, and then it is done.

It may not be easy, but it is simple.
Get moving.

Sometimes reevaluating *who* we are asking for help might take us to our final destination much more quickly. I truly believe that when we set our expectations up front, move toward our passion, pursue our dreams, and then put it out to the universe, we have the best chance of creating exactly what it is we are manifesting.

KEY TAKEAWAY

When we neglect to set expectations for a meeting, task, or other event in our life, career, or work, we are setting ourselves up for failure. Even beginning a new job is a great opportunity to set expectations in writing and ensure everyone is on the same page. This knowledge is definitely worth putting into practice now.

I would love to hear your story and answer your questions! To continue the conversation, join me wherever you are:

Twitter @_heathermonahan using #BAK
Instagram @heathermonahan using #confidencecreator
Linkedin @theheathermonahan using #overcomeyourvillains

CHAPTER 25

Things Don't Happen Overnight

"Real knowledge is to know the extent of one's ignorance."

—CONFUCIUS

One of the crazy things I've learned now that I'm on my own is that I will not know what my path is or what my next move is until I take action and just start moving forward. And one of the problems I've had when creating my own path is that things don't happen as quickly as I would like.

Back when I was in corporate America, I knew how long things would take to get done. I knew what the sales cycle was. I knew when my next budget was due. I knew how long it would take to get the next promotion. I could piece it together easily because everything was on someone's calendar.

Now that I'm on my own, however, I don't really know what's happening next or when it's going to happen—I'm creating it as I go. It's kind of like building an airplane while you're flying it. Sometimes the timelines get a little foggy, and as a result, things don't happen soon enough, which can be very frustrating.

If you get frustrated like I do when things don't happen as soon as you want or expect them to, here's my advice: just hang in there. Patience is a virtue I have not yet mastered.

In my experience, 97 percent of people will give up and will go to work for the 3 percent who didn't give up. That's true in most anything in your career or business, whether you're in your job trying to get promoted or you're focused on doing something on the side. Don't give up on it because you never know how close you are. Here's an example:

Ed Mylett is a super successful entrepreneur who lives in Laguna Beach, California. When I booked him for my podcast, I decided to do an in-person interview and flew out to LA. I always recommend going face-to-face on anything important. The opportunities you create when you are physically with someone are priceless. Ed and I were hanging out and talking after the show—I showed him my TEDx Talk and asked him what he thought.

He said, "Listen, you're a really strong speaker—you need to be speaking more and getting paid more." Wow. I liked Ed's vote of confidence.

So we started strategizing about exactly how I could make that happen, and Ed was super helpful. He said, "I want you to write down this platform. It's called Let's Engage, and I'm on it. This thing is right up your alley, Heather. It's got a lot of motivational, inspirational speaking opportunities. I think you need to be there."

Well, I took a ton of notes that day.

After I returned home to Miami, I jumped onto the Let's Engage platform. I decided it was worth exploring further so I spoke with the founder. We had an amazing call—we just hit it off. And, coincidentally, he happened to have an appointment to see Ed Mylett the very next day. The timing turned out to be perfect because he was planning to talk to Ed about me. You just never know what kind of good things can happen for you when you take a chance by picking up the phone and putting yourself out there.

Sure enough, Let's Engage decided to put me on their platform—they even decided to run ads for me on their own dime. All this happened because I made a personal connection with Ed Mylett. I took the time and spent the money to meet with him in person, and it was a game changer for me.

Cut to a year ago, when I was introduced to the president of one of the largest speaking bureaus in the country. He wasn't interested in picking me up at that time because they were more into booking political speakers and not business or motivational speakers. He just didn't feel I was the right fit at the time for what they were doing. But I decided to keep in touch with him anyway, and over a year's time, we forged a friendship.

One day, out of the blue, he sent me a note:

> Hey Heather, I was in California and I met this speaker agency that works with Brené Brown and a bunch of other female business, inspirational, and motivational speakers. I feel like you could be an ideal fit for them because Brené Brown is already booked out for the next year solid. When they get requests for her, they could hand them to you instead, creating a new revenue stream for the agency. It just aligns really well. What do you think?

I learned a very important lesson from this. While I might not have been the right fit for what he was doing when we were first introduced, by staying in touch, we built a relationship that led to a potentially incredible new opportunity for me.

Sometimes we might think, "Oh, I don't need to go to this meeting," or "I won't bother taking the time because who knows what will come out of it." That's the wrong attitude. It's an attitude of scarcity and not abundance. To succeed in life, you've got to invest in yourself. You've got to grab every opportunity you can and see where it takes you.

I have built everything in my own life off of that philosophy.

I will show up.

I will follow through.

And yes, sometimes nothing happens. But sometimes something great happens, and if you're not putting yourself out there—day after day after day—then you'll never get where you have the potential to go.

Here's another example. I've been going back and forth with Kim Gravel on a clothing line concept for HSN now for months. And it's funny. I always feel like I'm driving that woman crazy because I'm texting her all the time, I'm shooting her emails, I'm commenting on her social media. (By the way, that is the *best* way to get a hold of somebody and get their attention.) I'm always trying to stay top of mind with her—we've created a beautiful visual presentation.

One day, someone commented on my social media, "Heather, I wish you had a clothing line because I would buy it." And I said, "Oh my gosh, yes, I'm working on it." And I jumped right on Kim's text thread and said, "Is there any way we can talk?" and she called me right back.

Not giving up is absolutely critical to achieving your goals—and your dreams. You might be worried that you're annoying someone, but doing it in a positive and supportive way is really the key. It turns out Kim had her own things going on, which we all do. She had been super busy over the holidays, but when her schedule cleared out a bit, she gave me some constructive feedback on my presentation. I redid it and got it right back to her.

I always believe in the octopus strategy for revenue, having multiple streams going all the time. If one stream falls down for any reason, you'll be fine because you have other streams to replace it. And remember, good things don't always happen overnight. Sometimes they do, but be ready to keep plugging away at your goals until you reach them.

Don't give up! And stay tuned on the clothing line. We got another no from HSN, but that doesn't mean it's the end. It simply means we are in the middle of the story. Let's keep going.

KEY TAKEAWAY

Going all in on one idea may seem like a smart strategy—you will be completely focused and put all of your time and energy into something. That is, until that idea doesn't pan out or the platform it runs on disappears. Taking time to do a good job on a project makes sense. But once you have moved it forward, it is essential to get other balls up in the air too. Business is a numbers game. If you have just one pitch or idea out there, the probability is good it may not work out. If you throw ten balls up in the air, you have improved your odds immensely. Envision an octopus as your revenue strategy in order to ensure future growth.

Adaptability and making a commitment to change and evolve are your keys to survival. Knowledge is a powerful thing when put into action.

I would love to hear your story and answer your questions!
To continue the conversation, join me wherever you are:

Twitter @_heathermonahan using #BAK
Instagram @heathermonahan using #confidencecreator
Linkedin @theheathermonahan using #overcomeyourvillains

CHAPTER 26

What Will Your Legacy Be?

"Gaining knowledge is the first step to wisdom.
Sharing it is the first step to humanity."

—UNKNOWN

Recent years have been challenging for so many. There has been so much loss of life, so much disruption—it has seemed to affect everyone in some very personal way. In the middle of the pandemic, a very dear friend of mine passed away. No matter what the situation, losing someone special to you is devastating.

Years ago, as a young up-and-coming manager in radio, Bob McCurdy took me under his wing and made time to work with and mentor me. Over the years, he would share his research and insights with me, and I appreciated every minute of it.

Years later, when a leadership transition occurred at his company, Bob found himself unemployed. He called me and asked if I wanted a consultant, and I jumped at the chance. I was so excited to get the opportunity to work together. At six foot seven, Bob was a very tall, poised, smart, kind man, and I felt lucky to have him on my team. The first chance I got, I brought him on full-time as my right hand.

Over the years, working together, things would typically go the same way whenever we sat down to meet. We would go over the pressing work issues, and then I would shift the conversation to revenue growth, minimizing churn, new product launches, new business development, and on and on. Inevitably, he would stop me: "Yes. That's all really important stuff, but now it's time to talk about *legacy*."

Bob had much more experience than I did and was older than me. He was much wiser than I was then or am now, and he had reached a place in his life where he had kind of figured it all out. He had tremendous success in his basketball career and then as a corporate executive and as a husband and father. He had made friends, lost friends, grown companies, seen companies taken over, had successes with his peers, and fallouts with them. Through it all, Bob had a family he loved.

Bob loved to talk with me about leaving footprints in the sand. I would laugh and wonder what the heck he was talking about until he did it so frequently and with such a kind and loving approach that I knew he really wanted to impart his wisdom to me. This was much bigger than revenue growth and minimizing churn and new product launches.

He wanted my time with him to be meaningful.

We grew close over the years, and he knew of my son's love for basketball. The year I was born was the same year Bob was the nation's leading scorer at the University of Richmond. He had been selected in the eighth round of the NBA draft in 1975, only to be injured and never able to take the court. One day, I opened up a letter at home, and there were two tickets to the NBA All-Star Game in Toronto and a note from the Clippers coach to my son.

Bob had taken the time and asked for the favors and made the calls and annoyed the people to get my son a letter from an NBA coach and nab us tickets to an impossible event to attend—an event and experience my son would remember for the rest of his life. There were no words to express my gratitude.

All he would say in response to my thanks was, "Footprints in the sand."

It wasn't too long after the all-star game that Bob shared with me he might be sick. If you knew Bob, it was impossible to think of him as sick. He never complained and he always looked so healthy and strong. But you never really know what is going on in someone else's life. He would share bits and pieces with me as he began treatment. Every time we talked, he reminded me of the importance of legacy and leaving footprints in the sand.

When I was fired, Bob was one of the few people from the company who would call me. If the calls went to voicemail, he would leave messages checking in on me. He never gave up on me. Even knowing he could have been scrutinized by management for staying in touch with me, he didn't care. There are very few people from that time in my life who have consistently showed up for me and put our friendship first. As I said, he knew what mattered to him. In a cut-throat business in which most people were laser focused on getting *themselves* ahead, he was concerned about *me* and the footprints in the sand.

In April, Bob said on the phone, "Kiddo, I am going to send you something I've been working on. I think I have a book that may add some value to future generations and might help them too. Check it out. It's really rough but let me know what you think."

Bob didn't live to bring his book to light.

When I got the message he had passed, I immediately thought of how he had affected me, my son, and my perspective. I thought about his legacy and the footprints in the sand he had left for me and for so many others.

"Nothing is more important than health, other than your kids."

"Legacy is everything."

"Be sure to leave your footprints in the sand."

I thought about how much he loved his wife and his kids and all of the amazing memories they have with him. I thought of how he was gone too soon.

As I sat on my couch sobbing at the loss of someone so good, I realized that while he might not have been able to bring his book to life, maybe there was a way I could. I realized that I am part of the legacy that Bob has left behind. And I am following his footprints in the sand.

I'm so blessed to be launching my book with HarperCollins Leadership, and I can make this promise to Bob and to you: Bob's legacy will live on within me and this book for generations to come.

To my friend, my mentor, and my coach, your legacy will live on in me, and I promise I will make you proud.

What will *your* legacy be?

Before we finish the part on knowledge, I want to share my observations on the importance of the knowledge you access and curate.

Many people make excuses about not having time to access new knowledge, but that simply is not true. We all make time for priorities in our lives. I also guarantee that you either scroll thru Netflix or the news or something else that isn't helping your knowledge base and could easily be replaced with uplifting TED Talks or podcasts.

In addition, we need to curate and make better choices about the knowledge we let into our minds. That includes the people we share our concerns and dreams with and the people we follow on social media. Choose to access knowledge and people that lift you up and encourage you versus those that try to put others down or hold you back. If you can't find a mentor in your workplace or within your network of social contacts, you can find one online who can inspire you from afar.

I would rather eliminate people from my life who don't respect me and want me there than smile and grit my teeth sitting with those who stab others in the back. Knowledge comes from many places — choose yours wisely and intentionally. And always fire your villains to set yourself up for takeoff.

I would love to hear your story and answer your questions!
To continue the conversation, join me wherever you are:

Twitter @_heathermonahan using #BAK
Instagram @heathermonahan using #confidencecreator
Linkedin @theheathermonahan using #overcomeyourvillains

Pursue Your Dreams with a Growth Mindset

It's hard to try something you've never done before. After all, many of our fears are rooted in uncertainties. That's why people tend to stay in their comfort zones, to avoid risks. If we always pick comfortable situations, however, we cannot welcome new adventures and learn from the experience. We need to adopt a growth mindset and find the courage to go out there and see what life has to offer.

Besides, I need to remind you that your "comfort zones" really aren't that at all. They are really your "familiar zones." That was a big epiphany for me, and I want you to grasp it too.

When I was in corporate America, working side by side with my villain, I saw that situation as my comfort zone. Boy, was I wrong. I didn't anticipate that I could be fired. I also didn't recognize that there was nothing comfortable about it. Back then, my hair was falling out, and my stress was so bad I would cry at night.

What that situation should have been more accurately labeled as was a "familiar nightmare," not a comfort zone. Let's call things what they really are. Comfort zones are what you are used to and what you have lulled yourself into believing are safe.

Get ready for it: They are *not* safe, and they are *not* comfortable. They are only *familiar*. Just because something is familiar doesn't mean it is good enough for you.

In this exercise, you will learn how the difficulties in your life have made you stronger and wiser. You'll also get to understand the importance of a support system, a growth mindset, and the visualization of goals in the pursuit of your dreams. This exercise was inspired by my interview with Colin O'Brady, a world record–holding explorer and one of the world's best endurance athletes. His accomplishments include a solo crossing of Antarctica, the world's first human-powered crossing of Drake Passage, summitting Mount Everest (and the highest peaks on every other continent), and setting four mountaineering world records.

You don't have to cross Antarctica solo as Colin O'Brady did. You have your own Antarctica, but do you know what it is? What is your big goal?

ACTIVITY:
SET YOURSELF UP FOR SUCCESS

What's your Everest? Visualize your aspirations below.

_____

_____

_____

_____

How important is it to visualize your goals?

_____

_____

_____

_____

What are the things that you're doing or should be doing to reach your Everest? How will you achieve your ambition?

_____

_____

_____

_____

What are the things stopping you from taking that leap? How will you respond to the doubts in your mind that hinder you from pursuing your passion?

_____

_____

_____

_____

Friedrich Nietzsche, the German philosopher, famously said, "That which does not kill us makes us stronger." Were there challenges in your life that you had to overcome and pushed you to be wiser and stronger? How did they change your behavior and decisions for the future? Share your story below.

_____

_____

_____

_____

It is essential to have a reliable support system to encourage you when life gets tough. Who is your support system? How do they help you continue your trek to your dreams?

_____

_____

_____

_____

What is a growth mindset, and why is it important? Can you say that you have a growth mindset?

_____

_____

_____

_____

Were there moments in your life when you had to adapt to survive or finish a task? How vital is adaptability in pursuing your dreams?

_____

_____

_____

_____

Is competition beneficial? How does it help you elevate your performance?

_____

_____

_____

_____

Are there new things you want to try or past experiences you wish to pursue further? What are they?

_____

_____

_____

_____

Are you afraid to attempt new adventures? Why are some people afraid of trying new things?

_____

_____

It's not easy to pursue our goals; all humans feel fear and doubt their abilities and situations. But if you do not believe incredible things will happen, you will not work as hard as you can. You have to be the first person to believe in your dreams. Make a promise statement below telling yourself you will achieve great feats in your life. You can do it!

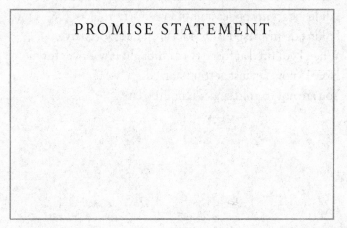

PROMISE STATEMENT

WHAT YOU'LL LEARN FROM THE EXERCISE

This exercise allows you to visualize your dreams. Visualization of your goals is crucial as it will help you to stay sharp and motivated. Moreover, if you can't envision your dreams, then you can't expect other people to help you achieve them. You have to be in charge of your future. The world doesn't owe you anything, and no one will offer you a free pass. Your first step is to visualize it for yourself.

We all encounter adversities—even the people you admire. But your heroes turn those difficulties into stepping-stones to reach their goals. Setbacks shouldn't stop you from doing what you love. No matter how heavy the blows are, you will be able to stand your ground as long as you work hard and believe in yourself.

In this exercise, you listed the people who you believe are your support system. It is vital to surround yourself with people who believe in your potential and dreams. There will be times when quitting would be the easy choice. But there's strength in knowing you have people rooting for you—and people willing to have uncomfortable conversations with you so you can continue to learn and grow.

As *you* grow, remember this:
I didn't write my first book until I was forty-three.
I didn't start my podcast until I was forty-four.
I didn't do my first TEDx Talk until I was forty-five.
When I got fired at forty-two, I thought it was over for me.
Now I know I'm just getting started.
You are not too old, and it is not too late.

Acknowledgments

I would like to thank every person who has cheered me on along the way and believed in me on the days when I didn't believe in myself. No one succeeds alone, and that includes me. I am eternally grateful for your support.

To Peter Economy, my editor: Thank you so much for making this process fun. Thank you for working with me even though we got fourteen noes because on lucky number fifteen we got a yes! Thanks for talking me off the ledge multiple times during this process as my wise friend.

To Jill Marsal, my agent: Thank you for guiding me through this very new and sometimes confusing process. Thank you for explaining things to me, and mostly thank you for being my advocate whenever I needed you.

To John Westman: Thank you for seeing value in me and giving me the opportunity to teach Professional Sales & Sales Leadership with you at Harvard.

To the *LadyGang*: Thank you for encouraging me into podcasting by bringing me on your show!

To Dr. Drew: Thank you for being so open and helpful in explaining why it was important for me to share my story. I am eternally grateful.

To Lauren Russo: Thank you for being my advocate and champion. The introductions and opportunities you have afforded me have been life changing. You are the epitome of a woman who supports other women.

To Sara Kendrick, my publisher at HarperCollins Leadership: Thank you for being so real with me and explaining things and advising me. I am so lucky to work with you!

To iHeart Radio: Thank you for bringing me on countless shows and highlighting my work even though I used to be your competitor.

To Gary Vaynerchuck: Thank you for being the first guest on my podcast and for all of the love and support you showed and continue to show me on social media. I am so grateful.

To James Altucher: Thank you for having me on your show and putting me on the map. Your kindness and help have meant so much to my success.

To Amy Morin: Thank you for coming on my show and having me on yours, and more importantly for your help with my TEDx Talk and your friendship.

To Jesse Itzler: Thank you for your encouragement and support and for green-lighting the opportunity to interview you and Sara onstage!

To Ed Mylett: Thank you for being on my show and for helping me with ideas and introductions and for your daily inspiration. And yes, thank you for having me as a guest on your show. Even though I haven't been on yet, I am sure you will have me on when this drops!

To Chris Voss: Thank you for being a guest on my show and for the countless fabulous people you have sent to me. Thank you for your advice when I had a friend in trouble. Thank you for being a great friend.

To Jamie Kern Lima: Thank you for being a guest on my show and for paving the way for females to succeed as a women who supports and drives forward for other women. Yes, I Believe It!

To Scott MacGregor: Thank you for being my ride or die. Thank you for always creating opportunities for me and being such an advocate. There are no words.

To DB: Thank you for always believing in me, supporting me, and pushing me to keep going. I am forever grateful to you.

Thank you to all of my friends and family: Your help and encouragement mean the world to me!

To the woman who fired me: THANK YOU, THANK YOU, THANK YOU!

To anyone who is pissed their name is not here: I am under deadline and this is stressful, so bring your book over and I will write it in personally for you. If you don't know me well enough to come over, then you can't be pissed.

I need to practice what I preach and just ask:

If you could please tell your friends about Overcome Your Villains,
leave a review and share it on social, I would be so grateful for your
help! Thank you!

Index

About Heather Monahan

With more than one million downloads of her podcast, Heather Monahan is a bestselling author, keynote speaker with the Harper Collins Speakers Bureau, entrepreneur, and founder of Boss In Heels LLC. Having successfully climbed the corporate ladder for nearly twenty years, Heather is one of the few women to break the glass ceiling and claim her spot in the C-suite. As a chief revenue officer in the media industry, Heather is a Glass Ceiling Award winner and was named one of the Most Influential Women in Radio in 2017. In 2018, Thrive Global named her a Limit-Breaking Female Founder. Real Leaders named her a Top 40 Female Keynote Speaker for 2020.

Her show—*Creating Confidence with Heather Monahan*, inspired by her first book, *Confidence Creator*—debuted in May 2019 on PodcastOne, the largest podcasting company in the US. Guests include entrepreneur icon Gary Vaynerchuk; hedge fund manager and bestselling author James Altucher; Ryan Serhant, star of *Million Dollar Listing NYC*; and Sara Blakely, founder of Spanx. The show topped the charts forty-eight hours after launch, and was listed as New & Noteworthy in the Business category on the Apple iTunes podcast charts.

Heather is a confidence expert who works with some of today's most successful Fortune 500 companies and professional sports teams to develop confidence in the workplace and on the court. She has been featured in *USA Today*, *Forbes*, PopSugar, *Business News Daily*, Refinery29, Dow Jones, Bustle, *Women's Health*, Thrive Global, and many others. In addition, she regularly makes television and radio appearances, including on CNN, Hallmark Channel, *Steve*, NBC News, iHeart Radio, CW South Florida, CBS Radio, Arise 360, and more.

At just twenty-five, Heather became an equity partner in Wilks Broadcasting, leading the company through a $27 million acquisition of radio stations in Saginaw, Michigan, and resulting in a $55 million sale of these properties in under three years. Heather took her expertise to corporate America, leading the sales organization for a major broadcasting company as VP of Sales. She was promoted to executive vice president and ultimately chief revenue officer of the company.

Boss In Heels, which Heather started in 2016, is a global community and lifestyle brand dedicated to helping others gain confidence and live their best lives. After twenty years in corporate America—shattering glass ceilings—Heather launched this site to share the insight and tips she had learned along the way to the C-suite.

In addition, Heather offers her life-changing Confidence Creator 101 online courses, which walk students through the steps required to create unlimited confidence and achieve their potential. This is the same curriculum Heather shared with BNY Mellon, Bacardi International, Google, the WNBA, MGM resorts, University of Miami Business School, and Harvard, among many others.

Heather is represented by APB Speakers and GDA Speakers, and she maintains a very active speaking schedule. She has served as a guest professor at Harvard University and University of Miami Business School and Law School. Heather is also a member of Florida International University's Advisory Council to further serve as a mentor and leader in the South Florida community.

Heather and her son, Dylan, reside in Miami.